The Cognitive Neuropsychology
of Schizophrenia

Contents

Prologue

In this short essay on the cognitive neuropsychology of schizophrenia I have considered only a very small fraction of the research on schizophrenia. The scope of my essay is indicated accurately by my rather unwieldy title. I have concentrated on the psychological aspects of schizophrenia and say little about medical, epidemiological or sociological aspects. There are many books covering these topics (e.g. Wing & Wing, 1982). Even within psychology I have restricted myself to a limited domain defined by the term "cognitive". My aim has been to describe the information processing abnormalities that underlie specific signs and symptoms associated with schizophrenia. I have therefore ignored many studies that have investigated psychological abnormalities associated with "schizophrenia" without consideration of particular symptoms. Much important work has been carried out on arousal, attention, memory and reaction time, but I have not discussed it here. These more general psychological studies of schizophrenia are thoroughly covered in John Cutting's book *The Psychology of Schizophrenia* (1989).

The cognitive approach in psychology is essentially theory driven. Theories are first presented, preferably in the form of "box and arrow" diagrams, then detailed hypotheses are derived and tested experimentally. I have adopted precisely this approach in my considerations of the signs and symptoms of schizophrenia. As this is a relatively new approach to schizophrenia, the result is stronger on hypotheses than it is on experimental evidence. However, my main intention in writing this essay is to convince the reader of the necessity for a cognitive approach to schizophrenic symptoms. My ideal reader will then go out and seek experimental evidence relevant to those hypotheses that he or she finds most interesting.

While I have only covered a fraction of the research on the psychology of schizophrenia, I have paid rather more attention than is usual in psychological essays to the brain. One of the fundamental assumptions of cognitive neuropsychology is that the behaviour and experience of brain-damaged patients can provide important information about the nature of the independent cognitive modules that underlie normal behaviour and experience. Given this assumption, it is, of course, perfectly possible for fruitful discussions about the nature of cognitive processes to proceed without any consideration of the nature of the associated brain systems. However, I believe that the study of people with brain damage may also help to map cognitive modules onto particular brain systems. Given this assumption, it is possible to use cognitive neuropsychology to give clues to the nature of the brain abnormalities associated with schizophrenia. This may be hopelessly optimistic, but I believe it is worthwhile to make the attempt. Furthermore, I believe that, over the next ten years, technical advances in functional brain imaging will make this approach to schizophrenia seem sound common sense rather than naive optimism.

I have tried to define all specialist terms when they first appear in the text and to avoid the use of footnotes. However, the reader cannot be expected to remember all this jargon. The most frequently used terms are the labels for the various signs and symptoms of schizophrenia and the names of various parts of the brain. Lists of positive symptoms are given in Table 1.2 and Example 5.1. Lists of behavioural signs are given in Tables 1.3 and 4.1. Examples of abnormal speech are given in Table 6.1. Rosalind Ridley has very kindly provided figures indicating the locations of the various brain components. These are shown in the Appendices.

This book represents my view of schizophrenia after working for 15 years in the Division of Psychiatry of the Clinical Research Centre, Northwick Park Hospital. I feel very privileged to have been a member of a group that has been highly influential in schizophrenia research. The setting at Northwick Park was, in many ways, ideal. Two aspects, in particular, I found important. First, my office was in the middle of a ward of acute psychiatric patients so that I never lost touch with the phenomena I was trying to explain. Second, I was part of a small and highly interactive group that included all the disciplines relevant to a complete explanation of schizophrenia, from molecular biology to cognitive psychology. I am very grateful to Tim Crow who created the

CRC Division of Psychiatry and who let me indulge in the fringe activity of "neuromythology". From Tim I learned that it is more valuable to develop a simple and testable theory, however unlikely, than mindlessly to collect data.

During this time, my principal collaborator in the domain of psychology was John Done. His role in developing the various models for schizophrenic signs and symptoms described in this book was at least as great as mine. His work in designing and carrying through experiments was crucial. Marilyn Stevens and Heidi Allen also played a major role in many of the psychological studies.

A psychologist who wishes to study schizophrenia is dependent upon collaboration with clinicians in order to get access to patients and, more important, to obtain detailed records of the mental states of these patients. I was most fortunate in having Eve Johnstone as my principal clinical collaborator. She taught me what I know of psychiatry and also that there is little point in having a clever theory unless you can also collect a lot of good data.

One of the main concerns of the Division of Psychiatry was to uncover the brain disorders associated with schizophrenia. When I first arrived I knew almost nothing about the brain. However, a short period of working in this new environment led me to believe that experimental psychology can reveal at least as much about how the brain works as analysis of urine samples. If I have acquired some knowledge about the brain and developed some ideas about how to link psychological processes with brain systems, then it is the consequence of daily coffee-time conversations with Rosalind Ridley and Harry Baker. I have benefited enormously from their experience and from their willingness to answer my questions about brain structure and function.

It is obvious that my studies of schizophrenia progress logically to brain imaging experiments in which the relationship between brain systems and cognitive processes can be studied directly. I have therefore been extremely fortunate to be able to move from the CRC Division of Psychiatry to the MRC Cyclotron Unit. This is one of the few centres where such studies can be carried out. I am grateful to all my colleagues at the Cyclotron Unit for their help and encouragement in the start of this new venture, but this story will be a different book.

Many people have read through various parts of of this book and have given me valuable advice. I list them here, not to suggest that they agree with what I say, but to indicate my thanks: Alan Baddeley, James Blair, Connie Cahill, Margaret Dewey, Karl Friston, Francesca Happé, Leslie Henderson, Eve Johnstone, Alan Leslie, John Morton, David Cunningham Owens, Richard Passingham, Josef Perner, Rosalind Ridley, and Daniel Roth.

I am especially grateful to my family, Uta, Martin, and Alex, who accepted without question that I should spend many evenings alone with my word processor. Martin read through the first draft of the book and made an heroic attempt to eliminate jargon and pretentiousness. Uta discussed all aspects of the book with me in detail. She also simplified my style, corrected my spelling, and, above all, provided the inspiration and the spur of her own work on autism. Without her this book would never have been written.

CHAPTER 1

The Nature of Schizophrenia

WHAT IS SCHIZOPHRENIA?

Case 1.1

PL first entered hospital at the age of 22. He had previously been taken to prison after a violent attack on his father, whom he believed to be the devil. During the preceding few weeks PL had become withdrawn and perplexed, making reference to religious themes. At interview PL described a mass of psychopathology. Abnormalities of perception were described, "Everything was very loud. I could hear the ash cracking off the end of the cigarette and hitting the floor. When I tapped the cigarette it went 'boom boom'. When I threw the cigarette on the floor it went thundering down". Isolated words and auditory hallucinations of water pouring out were present day and night, and PL described himself as holding his head a few inches off the pillow to alleviate this. He was sure he had been hypnotised by unknown persons and that this had caused him to believe his father was the devil. Olfactory and tactile hallucinations were also present, and in particular all his food "tasted the wrong way round". He believed he had "been crazy" and feared that he still was. He described with a measure of distress his loss of emotional response to things and people round him.

Case 1.2

SW was a 24-year-old mathematics teacher who was admitted to hospital after a four-week history of increasingly odd behaviour. He had left his flat and returned home, only to later leave and then return home again. SW took up sports and pursued them excessively, became uncharacteristically irritable and aggressive, unable to tolerate any music being played. He became preoccupied with incomprehensible life difficulties and expressed odd ideas, saying he should go to the police as his rent book was falsified and that he was teaching the wrong syllabus at school.

A few days after admission, SW became floridly psychotic, with grossly disordered speech[1]. His affect fluctuated from tears to elation over minutes. His general manner was distant, absorbed and perplexed. He expressed the beliefs that television and radio referred to him and certain records on radio were chosen deliberately to remind him of his past life. He was convinced his food was poisoned and felt his head and genitals were compressed as a result of an aeroplane flying overhead. SW described thought insertion and thought echo and heard hallucinatory sounds of a klaxon, and occasionally single words.

There was a slow reduction of these positive[2] psychotic features over a four-month period of treatment with antipsychotic drugs.

Following discharge SW had severe disabling negative symptoms: a lack of spontaneity and volition, and poverty of speech. After a year, he returned to work. He remained free of psychotic features, but his family was well aware of his persisting defect.

1: see Table 6.1 for examples and definitions of disordered speech.
2: see Table 1.2 for definitions of positive symptoms.

These cases are from a large collection made by Fiona Macmillan and Eve Johnstone which are reported in Fiona Macmillan's MD thesis (Macmillan, 1984) and are reproduced by kind permission of the author. As these cases illustrate, schizophrenia is a devastating disorder that can occur out of the blue; it wrecks promising careers; it destroys personal relationships; it ruins lives. In a survey of over 500 patients previously diagnosed schizophrenic in Harrow, a relatively affluent area on the edge of London, it was found that less than 20% were in full time work and that more than 30% had attempted to kill themselves at least once (Johnstone et al., 1991). Gunderson and Mosher (1975) have estimated that the cost of schizophrenia, in terms of treatment, care, and skills lost to the community, is at least 2% of the gross national product, i.e. about £2–3 billion per year.

Case 1.3

HM, aged 47, was a plump, pleasant woman, with an easy social manner. One year before her admission she had begun divorce proceedings, but her husband died before these plans came to fruition. The proceedings were prompted by HM developing the idea that a colleague from work had an interest in her, and that this man had enlisted the aid of groups of people who observed her. He also organised radio personalities to make reference to their liaison. HM described this surveillance as due to both paranormal and physical forces and believed it to be protective; but she had at times been fearful and was concerned that a carving knife was missing from her home and that she was followed by private detectives. These ideas had continued unabated despite having no contact with the man concerned for the preceding year. HM was admitted and rapidly transferred to day care. She clung to her ideas and was still in day care eight months later.

The cases described above are typical of schizophrenia, and yet each case is so different from the next that it is difficult to say what they have in common. Schizophrenia is so varied in its manifestations and course that some (e.g. Boyle, 1990) have questioned whether it is a single entity at all.

Nevertheless, using modern classification schemes such as PSE-CATEGO (Wing et al., 1974) and DSM-III-R (American Psychiatric

---

Case 1.4

Prior to her illness, CR, aged 20, had left home and was contemplating marriage. The most striking feature at interview was CR's disorganised behaviour. She would sit for only moments in a chair and then wander round the room, picking up articles and occasionally sitting on the floor. Her limited spontaneous speech consisted often of abrupt commands to be given something. It was almost impossible to gain her attention. She repeatedly removed her dressing gown and made highly inappropriate sexual advances to the male staff, and then tore bits off a picture of a swan. She appeared neither depressed nor elated and moved slowly. She said that God talked to her, saying "Shut up and get out of here". When replying to an enquiry as to interference with her thinking the patient said "The thoughts go back to the swan. I want the cross to keep it for ever and ever. It depends on the soldier Marcus the nurse".

After 6 months in hospital, CR returned to her mother's home, and 14 months after her first admission remains there attending a day centre. She is now extremely lethargic with affective flattening and some incongruity.

Association, 1987), psychiatrists can reliably and consistently specify a group of patients whose illness may be labelled "schizophrenia" (Table 1.1).

Many epidemiological studies have been conducted using classification schemes of this type (see Hare, 1982 for a review). These studies show that schizophrenia is a surprisingly common illness with a life-time risk of approximately 1 in 100 people. This risk seems to be largely independent of culture and socio-economic status. In men the most likely age of onset is in the mid-20s, but the illness can occur in children as young as eight, and typical schizophrenic symptoms can occur for the first time in the elderly. The illness is equally common in women, but the average age of onset is a few years later than in men, that is in the early 30s.

The cause of schizophrenia remains unknown (for a review see Cutting, 1985), but it is generally assumed that it has an organic basis. There is strong evidence for a genetic component and some evidence that risk is increased by birth injury and by viral infection during pregnancy. There is no evidence that psychosocial factors can "cause" schizophrenia, except, possibly, in individuals already at risk.

In order to be diagnosed as schizophrenic the patient must report particular kinds of bizarre experiences and beliefs. Many of the symptoms involve hearing voices (hallucinations). These voices are described as, "discussing my actions", "talking to me", "repeating my thoughts". Commonly found bizarre beliefs (delusions) are that "others can read my thoughts", that "alien forces are controlling my actions",

Table 1.1

DSM-III-R definition of schizophrenia

The patient must have
- A) characteristic psychotic symptoms for at least one week
- B) social functioning below previous levels during the disturbance
- C) no major changes in mood (depression or elation)
- D) continuous signs of the disturbance for at least 6 months
- E) no evidence of organic factors (e.g. drugs)

Characteristic psychotic symptoms must include
- (1) two of the following:
  - (a) delusions
  - (b) prominent hallucinations
  - (c) incoherence
  - (d) catatonic behaviour
  - (e) flat or grossly inappropriate affect
- OR (2) bizarre delusions (e.g. thought broadcasting)
- OR (3) prominent hallucinations of a voice with content unrelated to mood.

(see Table 1.2 for definitions of these symptoms)

that "famous people are communicating with me", that "my actions somehow affect world events". Table 1.2 lists these symptoms, which are often called "positive" because they are abnormal by their presence.

More rarely the patient's speech becomes extremely difficult to understand and is described as incoherent. On the next page is an example of such speech recorded by Til Wykes from a psychiatric interview. I shall look more closely at language disorders in schizophrenia in Chapter 6.

We only know about the bizarre experiences and beliefs because the patient tells us about them (symptoms). In addition there are abnormalities in behaviour that we can observe (signs). For instance, the patient may show a reduction in spontaneous behaviour in many areas, resulting in poverty of speech, poverty of ideas, poverty of action, and social withdrawal (Table 1.3). These signs are called "negative" because they represent an absence of behaviour that is present in normal people. Reduction of spontaneous behaviour tends to become more marked with time. In the later stages of the illness the bizarre experiences and beliefs may no longer be much in evidence and only the

Table 1.2
The major positive symptoms associated with schizophrenia

Thought insertion	Patients experience thoughts coming into their mind from an outside source
Thought broadcast	Patients experience thoughts leaving their mind and entering the minds of others
Thoughts spoken aloud/thought echo	Patients hear their thoughts spoken aloud, sometimes just after they have thought them
Thought withdrawal	Patients experience their thoughts being removed from their head
Third person auditory hallucinations	Patients hear voices discussing them in the third person, sometimes commenting on their actions
Second person auditory hallucinations	Patients hear voices talking to them
Delusions of control	Patients experience their actions as being controlled by an outside force
Delusions of reference	The actions and gestures of strangers are believed to have special relevance to the patient
Paranoid delusions	Patients believe that people are trying to harm them

---

Example 1.1 (from Wykes & Leff, 1982)

Where did all this start could it possibly have started the possibility operates some of the time having the same decision as you and possibility that I must now reflect or wash out any doubts that that's bothering me and one instant what's bothering me an awful lot in my wisdom the truth is I've got the truth to tell you with mine signing here and as I am as God made me and understand my position and you'll listen with intelligence your intelligence works lit again and is recorded in my head

---

"negative" signs (poverty of speech, etc.) are present (see Cutting, 1985). Diagnosis of schizophrenia in these cases depends upon reports of positive symptoms present in earlier stages of the illness. Depending upon the definition of schizophrenia applied, between 30 and 50% of cases progress to this chronic deteriorated state within two to five years after first admission. Acute episodes with bizarre symptoms can still occur in these chronic deteriorated cases.

Table 1.3
Negative features associated with schizophrenia
(from Andreasen, 1985)

Affective flattening or blunting (athymia)
    unchanging facial expression
    decreased spontaneous movements
    lack of expressive gestures
    lack of vocal inflections

Alogia
    poverty of speech
    poverty of content of speech
    increased latency of response

Avolition-Apathy (abulia)
    poor grooming and hygiene
    lack of persistence at work
    lack of energy

Anhedonia-Asociality
    loss of interest in recreation
    loss of interest in sex
    inability to feel intimacy
    inability to form friendships

PROBLEMS WITH DIAGNOSIS

I have already referred to studies showing that, with careful training in the use of standardised interviews, it is possible to achieve a high degree of reliability in the identification of schizophrenia in terms of some standardised procedure such as PSE-CATEGO (Wing et al., 1967). This, however, is not diagnosis, but classification. Traditionally, making a diagnosis has implications about aetiology. As the aetiology (or cause) of schizophrenia remains essentially unknown, this traditional approach creates many problems.

Schizophrenia is one of the psychoses, those severe mental illnesses in which the sufferer is no longer fully in touch with reality. At the turn of the century, Kraepelin (1896) proposed a simplified scheme for classifying the psychoses. Schizophrenia, which he called "dementia praecox", was distinguished from two other kinds of psychosis. On the one hand, there were the organic psychoses, like Alzheimer's disease, in which a characteristic neuropathology, i.e. visibly altered brain cells, had already been demonstrated. Since, as yet, no characteristic neuropathology had been identified for dementia praecox, this was labelled a "functional", as opposed to an "organic", psychosis. The functional psychoses were distinguished from the organic psychoses in terms of the patients' mental state. In a functional psychosis consciousness remains "clear", while in an organic psychosis there is "clouding of consciousness". On the other hand, within the functional psychoses, Kraepelin distinguished dementia praecox from manic-depressive psychosis partly in terms of its symptoms, and partly in terms of its course over time. Dementia praecox showed a decline from which there was no recovery, while patients with manic depressive psychosis alternated between periods of illness and periods of normality. Kraepelin hoped that eventually different causes would be found for these two kinds of "functional" psychosis.

Later, Bleuler (1913) proposed a different classification scheme which was based on an attempt to understand the psychological basis of the symptoms of dementia praecox. Bleuler coined the term "schizophrenia" to capture the notion of the "splitting" apart of different mental faculties. For example, the symptom "incongruity of affect" implies that emotion and understanding are no longer properly linked.

One hundred years later, and after many other classification schemes have been tried, the situation is very little changed. A characteristic abnormality in brain cells has not been identified in any functional psychosis, and distinctions still depend on considerations of symptoms, time course, and outcome, with no independent criteria for validation of these distinctions. The majority of psychiatrists still believe it is important to distinguish between different kinds of functional psychoses, but the evidence for the existence of these discrete entities has been questioned (e.g. Crow, 1986). A major contribution of modern diagnostic classification schemes has been to make explicit the basis of diagnosis. The major problem for these schemes is how to classify patients who have bizarre experiences and beliefs, such as those listed in Table 1.2, but who also have marked affective changes (depression or elation). PSE-CATEGO classifies such people as schizophrenic while DSM-III-R does not. Currently, DSM-III-R uses the narrowest definition of schizophrenia and the one that is closest to Kraepelin's original concept. In addition to mental state, DSM-III-R takes into account the time course of the illness. Patients have to show a loss of social functioning to below previous levels and to persist at this low level for at least six months.

The only way to validate these essentially arbitrary definitions is to find some independent marker of schizophrenia, such as a characteristic neuropathology or a missing enzyme. Unfortunately, at present, no such marker exists. Currently there is much excitement at the prospect of finding a "schizophrenia gene". There is abundant evidence for a genetic component in schizophrenia (Gottesman & Shields, 1982). If a gene (or genes) could be found, this would provide an ideal external validation for the diagnosis.

I have already stated that one of the most intractable problems for the diagnosis of schizophrenia is that diagnosis is supposed to have implications about causal origin. In line with this approach, all the diagnostic schemes have in common a particular exclusion criterion; that there must be no obvious organic basis for the disorder. Thus, a patient with a mental state fulfilling all the criteria for schizophrenia will not be so diagnosed if there is any known possible organic cause, such as a brain tumour, porphyria (the disease from which King George III may have suffered), or drug abuse. Given that it is now widely believed that there is an organic basis to schizophrenia, I find this approach somewhat paradoxical. It has the implication that a patient can only be diagnosed schizophrenic as long as the organic cause of the illness is unknown. This problem will only be resolved if it can be shown that the majority of people diagnosed as schizophrenic have in common a specific organic aetiology. However, the patients excluded from the diagnosis because there is a known organic basis for their disorder may well provide important clues as to the physiological basis of the signs and symptoms of schizophrenia (Feinstein & Ron, 1990).

The approach I shall take in this book follows that of cognitive neuropsychology. This approach has been successful in other areas and will avoid the difficult problems associated with the diagnosis of schizophrenia. Cognitive psychology is essentially synonymous with what used to be called information processing psychology. Cognitive processes are the hypothetical computational processes that underlie all our behaviour and mental experience. Most of these processes occur outside our conscious awareness.

CLASSIFYING SIGNS AND SYMPTOMS

The main purpose of this book is to examine, and try to explain the major signs (behaviour) and symptoms (experience) associated with schizophrenia in cognitive terms. I believe that the nature of the symptoms and any organic "cause" (genes, viruses, birth injury, etc.) give clues to the identity of some final common pathway in the brain which is functioning abnormally. For example, certain schizophrenic symptoms can be "caused" by large doses of amphetamine (Connell, 1958). As the principal effect of amphetamine is to activate the dopamine system, this phenomenon suggests that the dopamine system might be part of a common pathway responsible for some of the symptoms of schizophrenia. Since I am trying to explain signs and symptoms rather than "schizophrenia", my enterprise will not be hopelessly compromised if the definition of schizophrenia is revised.

The signs and symptoms associated with schizophrenia are many and diverse. Certain specific symptoms such as "hearing voices discussing me in the third person" are very rarely encountered, except in schizophrenic patients (World Health Organization, 1975). However, delusions and hallucinations are observed in patients with affective psychoses (e.g. delusions of guilt) as well as in patients with schizophrenia. Furthermore, some signs, such as poverty of action, can be observed in depression and in disorders with a known organic basis such as Parkinson's disease (Wolfe et al., 1990). Nevertheless, these latter features are an important component of schizophrenia (Andreasen & Flaum, 1991). Many patients diagnosed as schizophrenic on the basis of bizarre, positive symptoms subsequently develop negative features and no longer show positive symptoms. Such patients are sometimes called "burnt out", or referred to as having "residual schizophrenia". On their own, however, negative features are not sufficient for a diagnosis of schizophrenia because they can be observed in other conditions.

There have been many attempts to define diagnostic subcategories of schizophrenia that differ in their clinical picture, or symptomatology (e.g. paranoid schizophrenia, hebephrenic schizophrenia, and catatonic schizophrenia). These categories have not proved very reliable or useful and are now little used. In this chapter I have distinguished between the positive and negative features of schizophrenia. This distinction has dominated schizophrenia research over the last ten years since the publication of Tim Crow's article in 1980. Crow's scheme was a breakthrough for two reasons. First he attempted to classify symptoms rather than patients. Second he tried to map different symptoms onto different underlying pathological processes.

Positive symptoms are defined as being abnormal by their presence and include hallucinations, delusions, and incoherence of speech. Positive symptoms respond to treatment with neuroleptic drugs and therefore may reflect an abnormality in the function of the dopamine system (see Chapter 2). Negative symptoms are abnormal by their absence and include flattening of affect, poverty of action, and poverty of speech. Negative symptoms are associated with cognitive impairment and enlarged ventricles and may therefore reflect an abnormality of brain structure (see Chapter 2). A list of the various features associated with positive and negative symptoms is given in Table 1.4

As Crow was concerned to classify symptoms (or rather pathological processes) rather than patients, in his scheme it is perfectly possible for a patient to have both positive and negative features. In the majority of empirical studies, this has been found to be the case. Ratings of positive and negative features are usually found to be uncorrelated and therefore independent (e.g. Mortimer et al., 1990). This implies that, in any particular patient, either or both features can be found. This is a very strong result, as there are reasons for expecting a spurious, negative relationship (i.e. if negative features are high, then positive features will be low). For example, patients with poverty of speech may not reveal their incoherence or tell us about their delusions.

Table 1.4
Crow's two syndromes in schizophrenia (after Crow, 1980)

	Positive	Negative
Characteristic symptoms	Hallucinations Delusions Thought disorder	Poverty of speech Flattening of affect Social withdrawal
State of illness	Acute	Chronic
Response to antipsychotic drugs	Good	Poor
Intellectual impairment	Absent	Present
Pathological process	Increased dopamine receptors	Structural brain abnormalities

A problem with Crow's scheme lies in the definition of the two classes of symptom as "abnormal by their presence" and "abnormal by their absence". For example, stereotyped behaviour is a common, though neglected feature of chronic schizophrenia. The patient repeatedly performs pointless acts or produces repetitive speech (see Example 6.2, p. 102). Clearly, in terms of surface manifestation, this is a positive symptom because such acts are abnormal by their presence. This classification does not fit well as stereotyped behaviour is associated with negative symptoms (see Chapter 4).

Peter Liddle (1987a) classified the signs and symptoms of schizophrenia on a purely empirical basis. He rated a group of chronic patients with stable symptomatology on a series of signs and symptoms taken from the Present State Examination (PSE) and from the scales developed by Andreasen (1985) and applied factor analysis to these ratings; he found three factors. The first of these he labelled "psychomotor poverty". This factor includes poverty of speech, flattening of affect, and motor retardation and is the same as Crow's negative type. Liddle's other two factors—"reality distortion" and "disorganisation"—are subdivisions of Crow's positive type. There is an obvious face validity in this distinction as reality distortion (hallucinations and delusions) reflects abnormal experiences, while disorganisation (incoherence and incongruity) reflects a positive behavioural disturbance. A number of other studies have revealed three very similar classes of schizophrenic feature (see Arndt et al., 1991). The results of a recent study are shown in Table 1.5.

The well known problem with factor analytic studies of this sort is that the factors you get out are entirely determined by the measures that you put in. For example, if the Krawiecka scales are used for the ratings of signs and symptoms, only two measures of experiential symptoms are included; hallucinations and delusions. Using such a

Table 1.5
Clusters of signs and symptoms in a population-based sample of 329 schizophrenic patients (Johnstone et al., 1991). The scales of Krawiecka et al. (1977) were used to assess mental states

Feature	Factor 1	Factor 2	Factor 3
Retardation	0.874		
Muteness	0.874		
Flattening	0.734		
Hallucinations		0.859	
Delusions		0.851	
Incongruity			0.880
Incoherence		0.268	0.731

scale will not reveal different clusters of symptoms within the experiential domain. In order to decide which signs and symptoms are to be rated and then clustered we need a theory about what clusters are likely. One of my purposes in writing this book is to propose such a theory, in which symptom clusters are predicted on the basis of underlying cognitive defects.

In organising this book I have chosen a classification scheme based on the surface manifestations of signs and symptoms, but avoiding the problems of Crow's distinction between abnormal presence and absence. I have defined positive symptoms (hallucinations, delusions, etc.) as abnormal experiences, while negative symptoms (poverty of speech, social withdrawal, etc.) are defined as abnormal behaviour. From this point of view, negative symptoms are more properly called signs. By this scheme, signs such as incoherence of speech and incongruity of affect (Liddle's disorganisation cluster) are classified as abnormal behaviour and grouped with the negative features. I shall discuss all these behavioural features in Chapter 4 and all the positive, experiential features in Chapter 5. I have considered abnormalities of language separately in Chapter 6. Language abnormalities are one of the few features of schizophrenia to have been studied intensively in their own right and may reflect a number of different underlying cognitive abnormalities. As I shall show, there are many different reasons for being incoherent. In Chapter 7, I shall put forward my own ideas as to how all these various features of schizophrenia might reflect different impairments in a single cognitive mechanism: metarepresentation.

EXPLAINING SCHIZOPHRENIA OR EXPLAINING SYMPTOMS?

Eve Johnstone has recently reported the results of a study in which a large group of psychotic patients (including schizophrenic, manic, and depressed patients) were randomly allocated to various drug treatments (Johnstone et al., 1988). In this study response to treatment was determined by symptoms rather than diagnosis. Thus positive symptoms such as delusions responded well to treatment with neuroleptics whether they appeared in a patient diagnosed as schizophrenic or as suffering from an affective disorder. This suggests that there is a common mechanism underlying symptoms, which cuts across diagnosis. This is a very heartening result because, as we have seen, diagnosis remains essentially arbitrary, while symptoms can be reliably assessed. This study provides support at a biological level for the proposal that it is a more fruitful research strategy to study patients with certain symptoms rather than patients in particular diagnostic categories (Bentall, 1990).

In other areas of cognitive neuropsychology patients have been grouped by deficit rather than causal origin or diagnosis. Thus in the study of amnesia, for example, the cognitive deficit may be the same, whether the problem derives from excess alcohol or a penetrating missile wound. It is possible to argue that the location of the lesion in the brain is irrelevant to our attempt to understand the deficit in terms of cognitive processes in the mind.

In the psychoses the key features are not objectively measurable deficits such as those associated with amnesia or dyslexia, but subjective experiences like hearing voices or believing your actions are controlled by alien forces. In this book I shall discuss various attempts to explain these symptoms in cognitive terms. Such symptoms are most frequently associated with schizophrenia. However, the same explanation could very well apply to these symptoms when they are found in association with other diagnoses. I shall devote little space to the many experiments which have examined cognitive processes in "schizophrenia" without relating these processes to particular symptoms.

In addition to suggesting which cognitive processes are relevant to the signs and symptoms of schizophrenia, I shall also consider whether it is possible to relate particular cognitive processes to discrete brain systems. This exercise presupposes that the signs and symptoms of schizophrenia are the manifestation of a disorder of the brain. In the next chapter I shall present some of the evidence for this assumption.

CHAPTER 2

Brain Abnormalities in Schizophrenia

My purpose in this chapter is to outline the evidence for believing that schizophrenia results from a brain disorder. A recent and detailed account of some of this evidence may be found in Kerwin (1992).

Kraepelin first defined dementia praecox—which we now call schizophrenia—in 1890. At that time neuropathologists were achieving remarkable success in relating abnormal behaviour to brain pathology. Alzheimer was observing the plaques and tangles that are found in the brains of many patients with dementia and published his results in 1907. These biological markers could then be used to define the type of dementia that now bears his name. It was therefore possible to distinguish between different syndromes that had already been defined on the basis of gross signs of intellectual decline (e.g. Alzheimer's disease, general paresis of the insane) in terms of independent neuropathological signs. In Kraepelin's time no such characteristic abnormalities had been observed in the brains of patients with dementia praecox or manic-depressive psychosis. Nevertheless, it was believed that brain abnormalities would soon be found. This has proved to be more difficult than expected. Neuropathologists searched diligently and abnormalities were frequently reported, but they were never replicated. Indeed, schizophrenia eventually became to be known as "the graveyard of neuropathology" (Plum, 1972). I have known neuropathologists to remark facetiously that it is easy to recognise the brains from schizophrenic patients because they are the ones which look normal.

Meanwhile various theories have been proposed in which the signs and symptoms of schizophrenia were seen as "caused" by abnormal childhood experiences rather than abnormal brain function (e.g. Kasinin et al., 1934).

It is not surprising that, in such a climate, many people came to believe that there was no brain abnormality associated with schizophrenia. Indeed so firmly was this opinion held that many psychological test batteries, designed to detect "brain damage", were validated by demonstrating that schizophrenic patients performed such tests better than patients with known brain damage (e.g. L'Abate et al., 1962).

There were two major reasons for the dramatic switch of opinion in recent years towards the belief that schizophrenia is essentially a disease of the brain. The first was the chance discovery of antipsychotic drugs and the subsequent demonstration of their association with the neurotransmitter, dopamine. The second was the development of quantitative rather than qualitative studies of brain structure.

THE DOPAMINE THEORY OF SCHIZOPHRENIA

The Discovery of Antipsychotic Drugs

In the late 1950s chlorpromazine was developed as an antihistamine for use in surgery. It was observed to tranquillise patients without rendering them unconscious (Laborit, Huguenard, & Alluaume, 1952). This drug was found to be remarkably useful in the management of schizophrenic patients (Delay & Deniker, 1952). The results were so dramatic that, in a very short time, treatment with chlorpromazine or similar compounds became the dominant treatment for schizophrenia throughout the world. This was not, of course, the first physical treatment for schizophrenia, but it was the first to be so obviously effective. Insulin coma therapy was used for many years before it became clear it had no value (Ackner, Harris, & Oldham, 1957). Electroconvulsive therapy was applied to schizophrenic patients before it was applied to depression. It is still used today, although the evidence for its value in schizophrenia is weak (Hirsch, 1982). In contrast many carefully controlled studies have shown that antipsychotic drugs definitely reduce the severity of schizophrenic symptoms (Davis & Gerver, 1978).

The Mechanism of Action of Antipsychotic Drugs

Little is known about how or why most drug treatments work. Initially this was also true for the antipsychotic drugs. The situation was changed by developments in neuroscience. The presence of the neurotransmitter, dopamine, in the mammalian brain was first reported by Carlsson and his colleagues in 1958. Subsequently, its mode of action and distribution in the nervous system was studied intensively (Andén et al., 1964). Neurotransmitters are at the heart of the mechanism by which information is passed across the synapse from one nerve cell to the next. A neurotransmitter (e.g. dopamine) is released by one cell and diffuses across the synaptic cleft to another cell, which has receptors that are sensitive to that particular neurotransmitter. Neurotransmission can be interfered with in various ways. One of these is to "block" the receptors. This can be done by giving a drug that occupies the receptors and thus prevents the neurotransmitter from stimulating them.

Techniques were developed that permitted the action of any drug to be studied in terms of its effect on various neurotransmitters. By this time many antipsychotic drugs had been developed, all with roughly similar effectiveness in the management of schizophrenia. In terms of basic chemistry these drugs differed widely. However, it was found that their therapeutic effectiveness was closely related to their ability to block dopamine receptors (Seeman et al., 1976). This result strongly suggested that dopamine receptor blockade was a necessary component of antipsychotic action on the symptoms of schizophrenia. A number of studies were then carried out to demonstrate experimentally that this was indeed the case. I was involved in one such study conducted at Northwick Park Hospital (Johnstone et al., 1978b). Flupenthixol is a drug commonly used with schizophrenic patients. It exists in two forms (isomers), which are normally given as a mixture. The alpha isomer is a powerful dopamine receptor blocker while the beta isomer is not, otherwise the two forms have very similar actions on various other transmitter systems. Forty-five acute schizophrenic patients were randomly assigned to receive alpha-flupenthixol, beta-flupenthixol or a control condition with an inactive drug (placebo). As Figure 2.1 shows, there was no difference in the effectiveness of beta-flupenthixol or placebo but, after two weeks, the group treated with alpha-flupenthixol began to show a significantly greater reduction in symptom severity. This result confirms that dopamine blockade is a necessary condition for reduction of symptom severity with drug treatment.

If blocking the dopamine system reduces schizophrenic symptoms, then we would expect that stimulating the dopamine system would increase schizophrenic symptoms. This indeed turns out to be the case. Connell (1958) has described how drug addicts who take large amounts of amphetamine sometimes present at the clinic with signs and symptoms indistinguishable from those observed in some forms of schizophrenia. Their most frequent symptoms are delusions of persecution and auditory hallucinations. Angrist and his colleagues

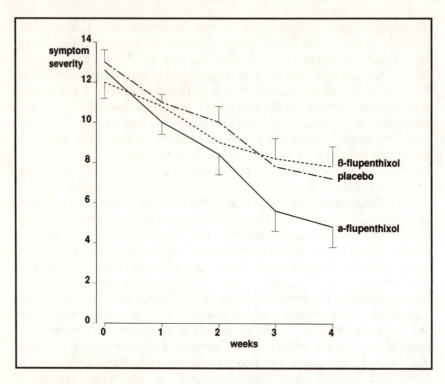

FIG. 2.1 Effects of a dopamine-blocking drug on total symptom severity in patients during an acute episode of schizophrenia (Johnstone et al., 1978).

(1974b) went further and studied the effects of amphetamine experimentally. They demonstrated that if normal volunteers were given large doses of amphetamine they would experience many schizophrenic symptoms. In the brain amphetamine causes the release of dopamine and its effects can be blocked by antipsychotic drugs (Angrist, Lee, & Gershon, 1974a).

At last it seemed that an organic cause of schizophrenia had been discovered. The simplest version of the dopamine theory of schizophrenia stated that schizophrenia occurred when there was too much dopaminergic activity in the brain (Randrup & Munkvad, 1972). However, this simple form of the dopamine theory of schizophrenia cannot be supported. Neurochemical studies of post-mortem brains and of cerebrospinal fluid have revealed no evidence of excess dopamine or increased dopamine turnover in schizophrenic patients (Crow et al., 1984).

There is some evidence, however, that the dopamine receptors in the brains of schizophrenic patients are supersensitive (Owen et al., 1978).

This would result in normal amounts of dopamine having excessive effects. Supersensitivity can also be caused by dopamine blocking drugs. When the receptors are blocked, and thus denied access to dopamine, they respond by becoming more sensitive. It is still not clear whether the supersensitivity found in the brains of schizophrenic patients is a marker of the illness or a consequence of drug treatment (Mackay et al., 1982). It is difficult to resolve the question using post-mortem material because brains mostly come from patients who die after many years of illness and prolonged drug treatment. Recently, techniques have been developed which permit the sensitivity of receptors to be measured in the brains of living subjects using positron emission tomography (PET). Using these techniques it is possible to examine patients at the beginning of their first episode of illness, before they have ever received drug treatment. Surprisingly, the results obtained using these techniques are still open to debate. In the USA receptors have been found to be markedly increased in drug-naïve schizophrenic patients (Wong et al., 1986). In Sweden, by contrast, receptor sensitivity has been found to be normal (Farde et al., 1987).

There is also indirect evidence against any simple dopamine hypothesis. It is clear from many drug trials that symptom severity is not affected immediately. In the trial illustrated in Figure 2.1, for example, it can be seen that the advantageous effect of the dopamine-blocking isomer on symptom severity does not appear for two weeks. Yet the effect of the drug upon the dopamine receptors occurs within hours (Cotes et al., 1978). Although dopamine is somehow relevant in the control of the symptoms of schizophrenia, its role must be indirect. Presumably there is some other system, more directly concerned with symptoms, which is modulated by dopamine. As yet no evidence permits us to identify this system.

Although antipsychotic drugs are remarkably effective at controlling symptoms in most cases, they are not the complete answer to the treatment of schizophrenia, and they are certainly not a cure. About 50% of patients relapse over a two year period in spite of treatment with antipsychotic drugs (Hogarty et al., 1974). Furthermore, there is very little evidence that antipsychotics alleviate the "negative" signs of schizophrenia (poverty of action , social withdrawal, etc.) in any type of patient (Angrist, Rotrosen, & Gershon, 1980). In the long term it is probably these features, rather than the positive ones (hallucinations, delusions, etc.) that would be the more important to treat, as their presence is linked to intellectual impairment and social decline.

There are also costs associated with antipsychotic treatment. Patients frequently complain of difficulties with thinking and concentration. These could well be associated with the sedative effects of these drugs (Hirsch, 1982). However, in Chapter 5, I shall suggest that subtle cognitive impairments are a necessary consequence of the mechanism by which dopamine blockade reduces positive symptoms. The precise nature of the cognitive changes brought about by treatment with antipsychotics are very difficult to disentangle from the effects of a reduction in symptom severity (Spohn & Strauss, 1989). On the other hand there are very obvious abnormalities of movement associated with this treatment.

There are two distinct types of effects of treatment with antipsychotics on the movement system. Many patients treated with these drugs show signs similar to those observed in patients with Parkinson's disease: tremor, stiffness, and an abnormal gait. These "Parkinsonian" side-effects appear soon after drug treatment commences and disappear when treatment is discontinued. They are a direct consequence of the effects of the drugs on the dopamine system (Marsden, Tarsy, & Baldessarini, 1975). We know that Parkinson's disease is a consequence of the loss of dopamine-containing nerve terminals in the striatum (Ehringer & Hornykiewicz, 1960). A similar, but temporary, lack of dopamine is produced by antipsychotic drugs. The Parkinsonian side-effects of these drugs are very common and many schizophrenic patients are given additional drugs (usually anticholinergics such as procyclidine) in the belief that these drugs will combat these side effects. As we shall see in Chapter 4, the link between schizophrenia and Parkinson's disease is of considerable interest. Parkinson's disease can be treated successfully with drugs which stimulate the dopamine system (e.g. L-dopa, a precursor of dopamine). Interestingly, this treatment sometimes causes psychotic symptoms (e.g. Celesia & Barr, 1970).

In addition to these Parkinsonian side-effects there is another kind of movement disorder associated with antipsychotic drug treatment known as "tardive dyskinesia" (Jeste & Wyatt, 1982). The most striking signs of the syndrome are strange involuntary movements of the mouth, tongue, and jaw (orofacial dyskinesia, buccal dyskinesia). These signs are widely believed to be the irreversible consequence of long-term treatment with antipsychotics. They are believed to continue and, perhaps, even to get worse when treatment with antipsychotics is discontinued. There is evidence, however, that these movement disorders were observed in chronic schizophrenic patients before antipsychotic treatment was available, and they can also be observed in patients today who have never been treated with antipsychotics (Owens, Johnstone, & Frith, 1982).

While we know very little about the role of the dopamine system in cognition, we do know something of its role in the control of movement from studies of Parkinson's disease. This knowledge can give us clues about the indirect role of the dopamine system in the control of the positive symptoms of schizophrenia. I shall discuss this further in Chapter 5.

STRUCTURAL BRAIN CHANGES IN SCHIZOPHRENIA

I shall now consider the second line of evidence that was responsible for the change of opinion about the biological basis of schizophrenia. As I have already stated, at the beginning of this century neuropathologists looked for and frequently found abnormalities in the brains of schizophrenic patients. However, these abnormalities were never found consistently and many brains from these patients appeared to be completely normal. Consequently many came to believe that there was nothing fundamentally wrong with the brains of schizophrenic patients. The steady trickle of reports suggesting otherwise was ignored. In the 1970s there was a technological breakthrough, which is continuing to revolutionise the study of the brain in man. Computerised axial tomography (CAT) permitted a detailed image of the brain to be obtained from a living subject. In particular it was possible to measure the size of the ventricles (the fluid-filled spaces in the middle of the brain; see Figure 2.2).

Simple measurement of the cross-sectional area of the lateral ventricles revealed them to be significantly enlarged in schizophrenic patients (Johnstone et al., 1976) Furthermore, for the first time in neuropathological studies of schizophrenia, this result has been replicated repeatedly (Gattaz, Kohlmeyer, & Gasser, 1991). Of course, the difference is quantitative, not qualitative. It is not the case that all schizophrenic patients have abnormally large ventricles. Rather it is the case that the mean ventricle size of a group of schizophrenic patients is larger than that of a control group matched for age, sex, and socio-economic status. At the most, perhaps 25% of chronic schizophrenics have abnormally large ventricles. Inevitably this quantitative difference was missed by the classical neuropathologists, who were seeking qualitative differences. From their point of view the discovery of enlarged ventricles in schizophrenia is not very satisfactory. The enlargement is certainly not unique to schizophrenia, it is also observed in a more exaggerated form in all kinds of organic dementia. Furthermore, the enlargement is not found in all schizophrenics. What, then, does it tell us about schizophrenia?

We might first consider whether enlarged ventricles are associated with a particular kind of schizophrenia in terms of signs and symptoms.

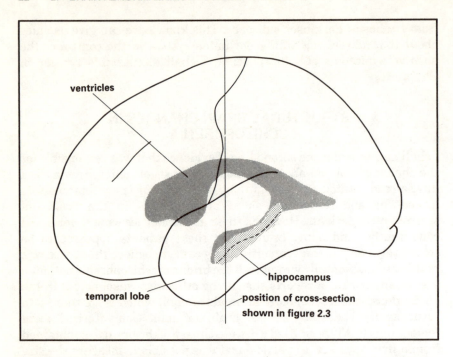

FIG. 2.2 Diagram of the human brain showing the position of internal structures—the lateral ventricles and the hippocampus.

We would expect them to be associated with a more "organic" picture. To some extent this is true. Enlarged ventricles are associated with involuntary movement disorders (Owens et al., 1985), a lack of response to drug treatment (Weinberger et al., 1980), and negative signs, rather than positive symptoms (Andreasen et al., 1982).

The enlarged ventricles must reflect some more specific brain abnormality, for example, a reduction in the size of a nearby structure such as the hippocampus, or a reduction in the numbers of a particular type of nerve cell. CAT does not give sufficiently detailed pictures to reveal what this abnormality might be. Attention has therefore switched back to post-mortem brains and to more advanced imaging techniques such as Magnetic Resonance Imaging (MRI). Studies using both these techniques have again confirmed that many schizophrenics have large ventricles (Nasrallah, 1991; Pakkenberg, 1987). In addition there is evidence that the enlargement is more marked in the part of the ventricular system that lies within the temporal lobe (the temporal horn) particularly on the left side of the brain (Crow et al., 1989; see Figure 2.3). Consistent with these observations, some studies have found that the hippocampus and the adjacent area of cortex, the parahippo- campal gyrus, are reduced in size in schizophrenia (Bogerts et al., 1985; Brown et al., 1986). Both these structures are part of the temporal lobe (Figure 2.3). Here again these differences are quantitative rather than qualitative. The differences may well represent a general reduction in the size of temporal lobe structures of all patients relative to the distribution in the normal population. The overlap between patients and normal subjects is such, however, that the size of these brain structures cannot qualify as "markers" for schizophrenia.

IS SCHIZOPHRENIA A NEURODEGENERATIVE DISEASE?

In neurodegenerative disorders, such as Alzheimer's disease, the ventricles become increasingly larger as tissue is lost. This is often the consequence of the progressive loss of a particular class of neurones; in the case of Alzheimer's disease, for example, those containing acetylcholine (Bowen et al., 1976). Therefore, if schizophrenia were a neurodegenerative disorder, we would expect to be able to observe the ventricles becoming larger as the illness progressed. We might also hope

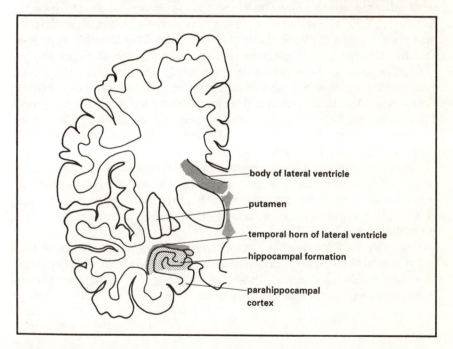

FIG. 2.3 Coronal cross-section through the human brain (one hemisphere only) showing structures in the medial temporal lobe.

to be able to identify the type of neurone that was being lost from neurochemical studies of post-mortem brains. Many such neurochemical studies have been carried out, but as yet no specific kind of neuronal loss has been reliably identified (Crow et al., 1984).

Likewise, repeated scans or scans of schizophrenic patients who have been ill for different lengths of time have not provided any evidence that the ventricles become progressively larger (Gattaz et al., 1991). There are a few instances where patients happened to have received scans well before the onset of schizophrenia. These cases have been found to have had large ventricles even at that early time, well before the onset of symptoms (O'Callaghan et al., 1988; Weinberger, 1988). These results suggest that schizophrenia is not a neurodegenerative disease and that brain abnormalities, including enlarged ventricles, precede the onset of the illness.

This suggestion is confirmed by studies that have looked for evidence of gliosis in the brain. If brain tissue degenerates and neurones die off then this is marked by gliosis, a sort of scar tissue. It is possible to measure the amount of gliosis in the brain, thus permitting a direct test of the hypothesis of degeneration. Although the brains of some schizophrenic patients may show evidence of gliosis most do not (Roberts & Bruton, 1990). Furthermore, even brains with enlarged ventricles may show no sign of gliosis (Bruton et al., 1990). This strongly suggests that the enlargement is not a consequence of a degenerative process.

On the basis of these results it is currently believed that the brain abnormality associated with schizophrenia occurs very early (e.g. before birth) and reflects a neurodevelopmental disorder (Murray & Lewis, 1987), that is, "a disorder in which early, fixed pathology becomes manifest clinically during the normal course of maturation of the brain" (Breslin & Weinberger, 1990). This idea fits in well with the assumption of a genetic basis, but does not exclude other biological causes that affect early development. There is, as yet, no agreement as to the nature of this abnormality. A major problem for this proposal is to explain how it is that the cognitive consequences of this brain abnormality are manifested so late in life.

Given that schizophrenia is associated with an abnormality of the brain, one of the primary concerns in the rest of this book is to consider how to relate the various signs and symptoms of schizophrenia to disturbances in particular brain systems.

CHAPTER 3

Linking the Mind and the Brain

In this chapter I shall first try to justify my belief in the importance of explaining the signs and symptoms of schizophrenia in terms of cognitive processes. I shall then consider some of the major practical problems confronting anyone attempting to develop a neuropsychology of schizophrenia.

SOME PHILOSOPHICAL PROBLEMS

How can we start to link the signs and symptoms of schizophrenia to an abnormality of brain function? This question requires a theory for relating mind to brain and thus steps into territory over which philosophers have long fought without reaching any resolution. Almost certainly these philosophical problems will dissolve or at least become radically reformulated as a consequence of new developments in cognitive science and neurophysiology (Dennett, 1991).

What is implied by my attempt to link the mind (which is the arena of schizophrenic symptoms) with the brain? For me the distinction between mind and brain concerns levels of explanation. Behaviour and experience can be explained in terms of mental processes or in terms of physiological processes. Both types of explanation are equally valid. Ideally the explanation can be formulated in such a way that each can readily be mapped onto the other. Philosophers call this identity theory, or, in a weaker form, parallelism. This attitude towards the mind–brain problem is much influenced by experience with computers. We can describe the operation of a computer in terms of processes within and interactions between central processors, memories, and response buffers. Alternatively, we can describe these processes in terms of electronics. We can happily cross the boundary between these two levels of description when we say, "here is the memory chip". Of course, this approach has difficult philosophical implications (Popper & Eccles, 1977). For example, if the brain has an equivalent mental description, then does all matter have an equivalent mental description?

My main concern in the first part of this chapter is to establish that certain causal explanations for schizophrenic symptoms are simply not admissible. For example, I think it is wrong to say, "thought disorder is caused by supersensitive dopamine receptors", or "hallucinations occur when the right hemisphere speaks to the left hemisphere via a faulty corpus callosum". The doctrine of parallelism requires that complete explanations of these phenomena can be made in either the mental or the physical domain. My two examples are incomplete explanations in either domain. Two incomplete explanations in different domains do not make up a complete description.

Let us first consider statements of the type "alien thoughts are caused by inappropriate firing of dopamine neurones". Let us assume that it is true that there is an association between alien thoughts and abnormal dopamine neurones. Nevertheless, the explanation is clearly inadequate. It says nothing about the nature of hallucinations nor the processes that underlie them. It does not say anything about the role of dopamine neurones within the physiological domain. Some might argue that, empirically, these details are irrelevant, because it is sufficient and important to demonstrate an association. This approach is very dangerous. In clinical research it is usually only possible to demonstrate association as opposed to causation. Thus, when you find that two things go together, say "family disruption" and "symptom severity", it is not immediately obvious which one causes the other. Something else might be causing both. Furthermore, with so many factors outside the experimenter's control, many spurious and irrelevant associations are likely to be found. This has certainly been the case in studies of psychosis. The history of biological psychiatry is full of "elephant's footprints in the mud" (Lancet, 1978); findings which have made a big impact at the time, but have then faded away. Examples, which I shall not reference, are the pink spot, platelet monoamine oxidase and the schizophrenia gene on chromosome 5. One way to reduce the influence of spurious associations is to adopt a theory-driven approach. This requires the construction of a detailed "story" in which associations are predicted rather than discovered (e.g. Crow, 1988).

A better, but still unsatisfactory way of making the link between mind and brain might be to say that "random, unnatural" firing of neurones lead to the patient having abnormal mental experiences. This is a dualist position in which the mind and the brain send messages to each other. This explanation is inadequate because it does not explain how the mind normally distinguishes between a natural and an unnatural mental experience. At the neural level there must be a mechanism that permits a distinction between unnatural firings and those that form a proper part of a larger scheme. Once we have explained how these distinctions are made we have, of course, returned to our parallel and alternative explanations in terms of mental or physiological events.

Let us now consider more complex arguments of the type "hallucinations are experienced because the right hemisphere is talking to the left hemisphere". This description also mixes up cognitive and physiological levels. The brain does not hear voices. Hearing voices is a subjective phenomenon lying within the realm of the mind. What the brain does is to process information, and there is a special part of the brain which processes the information relating to the auditory signals associated with speech. Some aspects of this information are processed in the left hemisphere only. There are many other specialised modules throughout the brain. For example in the visual system there are separate modules for colour, form, and motion (Zeki, 1978). Evidence for the existence of such modules can also be found in the domain of the mind (Fodor, 1983) and the two domains can be linked in terms of computation (Marr, 1982). All these modules need to communicate with each other. We could thus interpret the idea of the "right hemisphere communicating with the left hemisphere" in terms of communication between two such modules. The central question would still remain as to why internal communication between information processing modules should be interpreted as external speech. Furthermore, it is not at all clear why information processed in the right hemisphere should be interpreted as coming from an external source. However, as we shall see in Chapter 5, the inability to distinguish between "internal" and "external" may well be a crucial component in the understanding of certain symptoms of schizophrenia.

Looked at more closely, then, these explanations for the abnormal experiences of schizophrenia are metaphors. They put before us, in a striking form, the problems that arise when we have to cross the divide between mind and brain and consider how an abnormal brain can lead to an abnormal mental experience. My approach will be to develop as complete as possible an explanation at the psychological level. In parallel with this there should eventually be a complete explanation at the physiological level. Both explanations should be continuously modified so that mapping from one to the other is made easier. By searching for commonalities between the two domains, what we know about physiology will influence our explanation at the psychological level and vice versa. Figure 3.1 shows an example of hypothetical correspondences between the mental and the physical domains. This is based on a series of studies using positron emission tomography (PET) and attempts to map discrete cognitive processing modules onto circumscribed brain regions (Petersen et al., 1989). It is important to note that Petersen and his colleagues are mapping cognitive processes,

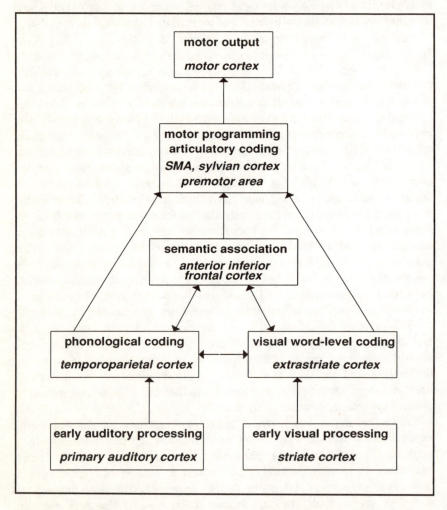

FIG. 3.1 A scheme for single word processing linking cognitive modules and brain regions (after Petersen et al., 1989).

rather than behaviour or mental experience. Performance of any particular word processing task requires at least four of the cognitive components illustrated in Figure 3.1. Mesulam (1990) has presented an even more ambitious mapping project, which goes beyond simple localisation and considers underlying neural networks and interactions between modules.

Given this approach to the relationship between mind and brain, there are two clear components in any attempt to specify the neuropsychology of schizophrenia. First, a description of schizophrenic abnormalities at a psychological level, and, second, a specification of how this description maps onto abnormalities at a physiological level.

Animal Models of Schizophrenia

A truly experimental investigation of the links between psychology and physiology can only be achieved in studies of animals. In such studies it is possible to intervene directly in brain function. It is therefore important to consider whether it is possible to have animal models relevant to the signs and symptoms of schizophrenia (Ellenbroek & Cools, 1990). Certain of the signs of schizophrenia can be studied directly in animals. Stereotyped behaviour has been extensively studied in animals and there is evidence that the dopamine system is implicated in this behaviour. I shall discuss these studies in Chapter 4. Abnormalities of social interaction, including social withdrawal have also been studied in animals and I shall discuss this evidence in Chapter 7. Obviously, those signs and symptoms which involve speech (poverty, incoherence) or subjective experience (delusions, hallucinations) cannot be studied directly in animals. However, if we can specify the cognitive processes that underlie these symptoms then it may be possible to study these processes in animals

Jeffrey Gray and his colleagues have focused on a process termed latent inhibition. If subjects have previously experienced that a certain stimulus is irrelevant, then they will take longer to learn that this stimulus is now associated with some important event. This delay in learning reflects latent inhibition. It has been shown that latent inhibition tasks are performed abnormally in patients with acute schizophrenia (Baruch, Hemsley, & Gray, 1988) and in animals treated with amphetamine (Weiner, Lubow, & Feldon, 1981). Gray et al. (1990) have put forward a detailed account of this model in which psychological processes are linked to brain systems very much in the way I am advocating in this chapter. However, it remains to be seen whether this account succeeds in relating latent inhibition to particular signs or symptoms of schizophrenia at either a theoretical or an empirical level.

The problem is that latent inhibition is not really a cognitive process, but a label for a particular type of task. There have been attempts to analyse the cognitive components of this task (e.g. Hall & Honey, 1987). Gray and his colleagues say very little about these components. Instead, they link latent inhibition to symptoms via concepts of stimulus relevance or "past regularities". For example, "over-attention" is explained as follows (Gray et al., 1990): "There is a weakening of the capacity to select for cognitive processing only those stimuli which, given past experience of similar contexts, are relevant ... defining relevance in terms of current 'plans' ". Hallucinations are explained as "intrusions into conscious experience of material from long term memory, this being attributed to an external source". These intrusions occur "in schizophrenia (because of) the lack of structure which ... characterises their sensory experience". Unfortunately, the cognitive basis of these formulations are too vague to be useful. The important link that is made between animal behaviour and schizophrenic symptoms is via task performance rather than underlying cognitive processes. This is an important attempt to model schizophrenia in the tradition of behaviourism, but it is essentially an argument by analogy. As I shall point out in the next section, such analogies can be dangerous even when relating schizophrenia to neurological disorders, let alone animal studies.

There are other models that are explicitly stated in terms of task performance. For example, pre-pulse inhibition, the reduction of a startle response to a stimulus if that stimulus has been preceded by a similar stimulus of lower intensity, has been found to be abnormal in schizophrenic patients as well as animals treated with amphetamine (Braff et al., 1978). Once such tasks have been related to specific schizophrenic signs or symptoms and analysed in terms of fundamental cognitive processes, then they may well provide powerful techniques for linking brain function to cognitive processes relevant to schizophrenia. In all these attempts to develop animal models of schizophrenia the starting point has been a paradigm developed with animals which has then been modified and applied to schizophrenic patients. In Chapter 7 I shall try the opposite approach. As I will show, there is reason to believe that the cognitive processes underlying metarepresentation are crucial in the production of schizophrenic symptoms. I shall therefore consider whether it is possible to study these processes in animals.

PROBLEMS IN STUDYING PSYCHOLOGICAL IMPAIRMENTS IN SCHIZOPHRENIA

There have been a great many experimental studies of the psychology of schizophrenia, but remarkably little agreement as to their significance, and repetitions of experiments have not always produced the same results. Some of the problems associated with the study of schizophrenia are simply a consequence of being ill. There are many consequences of having a chronic and debilitating illness, which must have an effect on psychological outcome.

Drug Treatment

The vast majority of schizophrenic patients are being treated, fairly vigorously, with drugs. We therefore have to consider whether drug treatment might result in cognitive impairment.   Schizophrenic patients often receive many different kinds of drug in addition to the ubiquitous neuroleptics. Some of these, particularly anticholinergics and the minor tranquillisers, can cause memory impairments (Frith, 1984). However, it is difficult to maintain that all the cognitive deficits shown by the patients are caused by drug treatments. Kraepelin's patients had never been treated with drugs, but he considered that they had a form of dementia. Ideally, we would like to study patients who are drug-free, but this is usually not possible. Even when such patients can be found in the acute stage of the illness, it is likely that many will be unable to participate in psychological experiments. It is also likely that the patients whom clinicians are prepared to leave untreated and who will cooperate while psychological tests are carried out are unrepresentative.

Institutionalisation

A similar problem concerns institutionalisation. Until recently, most schizophrenic patients who took part in psychological studies came from large institutions in which they had been living for a great many years. Undoubtedly, the way in which a long-stay institution is run can affect behaviour. In a study of several such institutions, Wing and Brown (1970) found that patients in the institution with the least socially stimulating environment were the most underactive, slow, and withdrawn. Such observations have lead to the belief that poor performance on psychological tests may be a consequence of institutionalisation rather than schizophrenia. Nevertheless, this is not sufficient to explain the degree of impairment shown by some patients. After the adoption of community care it has been found that similar degrees of cognitive impairment and negative features are seen in patients who are not in institutions (Johnstone et al., 1985; Leach & Wing, 1980). Furthermore, physically disabled patients living in long-stay institutions do not show such impairments (Johnstone et al., 1978a).

Control Groups

In principle the problem posed by drug treatment and institutionalisation can be solved by choosing the right control group. We cannot perform a true experiment with schizophrenic patients because we cannot randomly assign people to be schizophrenics or controls. However, we can try and find a control group that differs from the schizophrenic group only in that the controls are not schizophrenic. For example, if we believed that drug treatment had a systematic effect on performance, we would compare drug-treated schizophrenics with drug-treated controls. The same strategy would be applied to the problem of institutionalisation. Obviously, we are unlikely to find people who have lived in an institution and have been treated with neuroleptic drugs for 20 years and yet are not schizophrenic. Clearly the ideal control group does not exist. Nevertheless, for want of anything better, we will have to continue to do experiments in which we compare schizophrenic patients with unsatisfactory controls. This means that we must treat the results with extreme caution. In particular, we must be on our guard if we find performance impairments. Often, impairment will reflect some general deficit that is not specific to schizophrenia. This general deficit might be a consequence of some extraneous factor which, by chance, differentiates the schizophrenic patients from the controls.

Problems with Diagnosis

There is, however, an additional and major problem with such studies, which we constantly come up against. This concerns the definition of schizophrenia. As we have seen there is still no absolute agreement on the kind of patient that is a "true" schizophrenic. In addition, schizophrenic patients can differ widely in the type of symptoms that they currently manifest. Thus, early studies, in which all that is specified about the patients is a hospital diagnosis of schizophrenia, are very difficult to interpret. In more recent studies it is usual for the diagnostic criteria to be specified (e.g. DSM-III-R), but different studies may use different diagnostic criteria. Furthermore, diagnostic criteria are not sufficient for interpreting results. We also need to know the particular symptoms shown by the patient at the time of testing.

Diagnosis or Symptoms?

There is an even more fundamental problem. Demonstrating that schizophrenic patients have certain cognitive abnormalities does not "explain" schizophrenia. "Explaining" schizophrenia inevitably involves saying something about cause. This leads us back to the mind–brain problem. The aetiology of schizophrenia almost certainly involves abnormal brain development. Cognitive abnormalities can tell us nothing directly about brain structure and function, let alone brain development. What studies of cognition can "explain" is not schizophrenia, but schizophrenic symptoms. Thus we can say "he hears voices because of a fault in his central monitoring system". We cannot say "he has schizophrenia because of a fault in his central monitoring system". We might eventually be able to say "he has schizophrenia because of damage to the uncinate fascicle which subserves central monitoring, thus leading to hallucinations". It follows that what we should be demonstrating is not that schizophrenia is associated with certain cognitive abnormalities, but, instead, that certain symptoms are. Thus our experimental groups should be composed, not of DSM-III-R schizophrenics, but DSM-III-R schizophrenics with delusions of control, or whatever the target symptom may be.

By making symptoms rather than diagnosis the target of our investigations we are following the approach used by cognitive neuropsychologists in their studies of neurological patients. Most of these studies have been concerned with single cases. However, when cases are compared and combined it is in terms of the deficits that they show (e.g. short-term memory impairment) rather then the location of the lesion. In the case of schizophrenia, it is the symptoms that correspond to the deficit shown by neurological patients. It is the symptoms, then, that we must explain in terms of underlying cognitive processes.

Studying symptoms, rather than diagnosis, has a number of additional advantages. I just pointed out that it is almost impossible to find a non-schizophrenic control group that is properly matched for drug treatment and institutionalisation. This difficulty is much reduced if we compare schizophrenic patients with and without a certain symptom. Such groups can be more easily matched on factors such as treatment and length of hospitalisation.

Focusing on symptoms also avoids other problems associated with drug treatment. For example, if we studied "attention" in schizophrenia any abnormality observed might be due to effects of drugs, rather than the illness. It would therefore be essential to assess the effects of drug treatment on the same measures in normal volunteers. In contrast, if we study the cognitive abnormality underlying a particular symptom, then we know that the cognitive abnormality must be present if the patient still experiences the symptom. This will apply whether or not the patient is being treated with drugs.

LINKING PSYCHOLOGICAL ABNORMALITIES WITH BRAIN DYSFUNCTION

I have proposed that psychological studies would be more informative if we studied schizophrenic patients with particular symptoms rather than schizophrenic patients in general. We must now consider the question of how these psychological studies can give us clues about the nature of the brain abnormalities underlying these symptoms. A popular approach is by analogy with neurological patients. Many features related to schizophrenia can also be observed in neurological patients. Maybe these patients can give us a clue about the brain abnormalities associated with schizophrenia?

Core Features and Related Features

In most diagnostic schemes, all schizophrenic patients have to show positive symptoms (hallucination and delusions) at some stage of their illness. We might refer to these as the core features of schizophrenia. Having defined schizophrenia in such a way, it is clear that there are a number features that are often seen in association with this diagnosis. These related features are found in many schizophrenic patients, but not in all. Sometimes they appear later in the illness. At very late stages only these related features may remain, while the core features are no longer there. The reason that the presence of these related features is not sufficient for a diagnosis of schizophrenia is that they can also be observed in other types of patient. Of particular interest are those features that can be observed in neurological patients with known brain damage.

Negative Signs
A substantial number of schizophrenic patients either have from the outset, or later develop, negative signs. Negative signs include social withdrawal, poverty of speech, and lack of will. Some would argue that only those who do develop negative signs are "true" schizophrenics. Others have suggested that negative signs reflect a coping strategy for

dealing with positive symptoms (e.g. Hemsley, 1977). For example, if positive symptoms are due to excessive stimulation then withdrawal from all activities would be a way of reducing stimulation. There are two reasons that make it unlikely that negative signs are simply a secondary response to positive symptoms. First, negative signs can be present from the very earliest stages of the illness (Montague et al., 1989). Second, negative signs seem to be associated with structural brain changes (Marks & Luchins, 1990).

General Cognitive Impairment

In terms of their performance on standard IQ tests many schizophrenic patients show a marked decline from premorbid levels. Intellectual impairment is associated with negative signs and incoherence, but not positive symptoms (Frith et al., 1991b). How quickly this decline occurs is not clear, but it is probably fairly rapid, being largely complete during the first five years of illness. Sometimes the final level is extremely low, leaving the patient essentially demented. About 25% of chronic hospitalised schizophrenic patients are functioning at this level (Stevens et al., 1978).

Amnesia

Memory impairment is part of the general cognitive impairment shown by many schizophrenic patients. However, severe memory impairments can also be found in patients who achieve normal scores on IQ tests. (McKenna et al., 1990) These memory impairments do not resemble those associated with Alzheimer's disease but, rather, the amnesia associated with Korsakoff's syndrome.

Perceptual Problems

Amnesia is not the only circumscribed cognitive impairment that can be observed in schizophrenia. Paul Burgess, Tim Shallice, and I have, for instance, examined intensively a chronic schizophrenic patient who has a severe perceptual impairment in addition to a mild general cognitive impairment (Shallice, Burgess, & Frith, 1991). This patient achieves an abnormally low score on an object naming test. His perception seems to be abnormally dependent on detail at the expense of the whole. For example, he named a tassle as a man because there were lines in it resembling eyes and nose. This impairment is a very exaggerated version of a perceptual style often attributed to schizophrenic patients. It has been said that a schizophrenic patient "can't see the wood for the trees ... examines each tree with meticulous care" (Shakow, 1950). How many schizophrenic patients have perceptual impairments of this extreme kind is not yet known.

Involuntary Movement Disorders

Chronic schizophrenic patients often make peculiar movements. In particular they make strange grimaces with their lips and mouth. These movements are involuntary but do not seem to cause the patient any concern. For a time it was widely believed that these movements were caused by long-term treatment with neuroleptic drugs. However, similar movements were described by Kraepelin and others long before neuroleptics became available. It is now clear that some patients develop movement disorders whether or not they are drug-treated (Owens et al., 1982). Treatment with neuroleptics, however, may well make these movement disorders worse.

Incoherent Speech

About 16% of patients with a diagnosis of schizophrenia have incoherent speech (Andreasen, 1979). I shall discuss the nature of schizophrenic speech more fully in Chapter 6. For the purposes of my argument here, it is sufficient to note that incoherence is another related feature that is not found in all schizophrenic patients.

The core symptoms of schizophrenia and the cluster of related disorders can be conveniently illustrated by a Venn diagram (Figure 3.2). Some of the associated abnormalities are strongly related to one another. In particular, negative signs, movement disorders, and dementia (Owens et al., 1982). Some of the related disorders, such as amnesia and perceptual disorders, have not yet been sufficiently investigated for us to know about their relationships with other features. There are almost certainly additional associated abnormalities that have not yet been described.

I assume that all these cognitive and behavioural disorders map onto disorders of underlying brain systems. We might, therefore, expect a corresponding Venn diagram for brain systems. In other words, abnormality in a certain brain area or system results in the core features of schizophrenia (positive symptoms). If this abnormality impinges on additional regions which are related either by proximity or direct neural connections then other abnormalities will occur in addition to the core features.

Of course, the associated abnormalities of schizophrenia are found in other conditions as well. That is why they cannot be used as defining features of schizophrenia. However, in many cases the brain abnormalities underlying these other disorders are known. Maybe this knowledge about other disorders will give us clues to the brain abnormalities underlying schizophrenia. In Table 3.1 I have listed the associated disorders and the brain abnormalities that underlie them in non-schizophrenic patients.

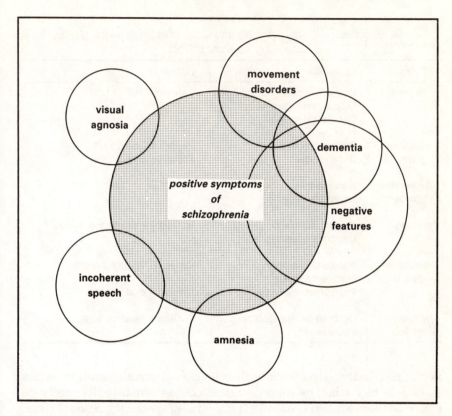

FIG. 3.2 Deficits associated with schizophrenia.

Almost all possible brain regions seem to be implicated in this table. Clearly this exercise has not helped us to specify a particular brain region associated with the core features of schizophrenia. Instead, it illustrates the difficulty of using analogy with neurological patients in order to increase our understanding of schizophrenia.

A NEUROPSYCHOLOGY OF SCHIZOPHRENIA?

A more refined version of the use of this analogy with neurological patients is provided by classical neuropsychology. A wide range of psychological tests have been applied to patients with neurological lesions. This has permitted psychologists to identify tests associated with various locations of damage. In the ideal case such a test is

Table 3.1

Deficits associated with schizophrenia and lesion sites in neurological patients showing the same deficits

Deficit	Lesion site	Reference
Dementia	Cortex (temporal, frontal) Hippocampus/amygdala Cholinergic system	Lishman, 1987
Negative features	Prefrontal cortex Basal ganglia	Hecaen & Albert, 1975 Kolb & Wishaw, 1985
Movement disorders	Basal ganglia Dopamine system	Jeste & Wyatt, 1982
Amnesia	Medial temporal lobe Hippocampus/amygdala	McCarthy & Warrington, 1990
Incoherent speech	Parieto-temporal junction/ arcuate fasciculus Right prefrontal cortex	Kertesz & Shephard, 1981 Alexander et al., 1989
Visual agnosia	Occipital-parietal junction/ splenium	Shallice & Jackson, 1988

performed badly by patients with lesions in a certain location, while lesions in any other location do not affect performance. As might be expected there are few tests with this degree of specificity. Nevertheless, there are now a substantial number of tests with a reasonable degree of localisation. There are many studies in which such tests have been applied to schizophrenic patients (e.g. Gruzelier et al., 1988; Kolb & Wishaw, 1983). The argument is, that if schizophrenic patients perform badly on a particular test, then they must have brain damage in the location associated with that particular test. It is striking that this approach has not led to any consensus about the brain abnormalities associated with schizophrenia. On the basis of such studies almost every part of the brain has been identified as crucially involved. Gruzelier and Flor-Henry (1979) favour a left hemisphere abnormality or a hemisphere imbalance. Cutting (1990) favours a right hemisphere deficit. Weinberger (1984) and Morice (1990) consider that the frontal cortex is implicated. Clearly there are problems applying classical neuropsychology to schizophrenia.

One problem with most of these studies is that they have used large groups of schizophrenic patients who almost certainly showed a wide range of different signs and symptoms at the time of testing. If different cognitive deficits are associated with different signs and symptoms then the mean performance of a heterogeneous group of schizophrenic patients will give a very misleading picture of the neuropsychological profile associated with schizophrenia.

Peter Liddle has attempted to overcome this problem by contrasting groups of patients defined in terms of his three syndromes (Liddle, 1987b; Liddle & Morris, 1991). These studies confirm that patients with different signs and symptoms do indeed show a different pattern of performance on neuropsychological tests. Tim Shallice, Paul Burgess, and I took this strategy to its extreme and examined the performance of individual patients on a very wide range of neuropsychological tests (Shallice et al., 1991). This study revealed a very variable pattern of abilities, none of which corresponded to any particular neurological syndrome. If schizophrenic patients failed on a very specific subset of tests this would be a very useful clue to underlying brain dysfunction. However, in practice, as this study confirmed, chronic schizophrenic patients are likely to be impaired on a wide range of neuropsychological tests. This makes interpretation particularly difficult. The neuropsychological approach is based on very carefully selected neurological patients who are impaired on a small subset of tests while remaining intact in all other spheres (Shallice, 1988). It seems that close analogies between the performance of schizophrenic patients and such neurological cases cannot be found.

I believe that there is a fundamental flaw in the approach of classical neuropsychology. What is sought in this approach is an association between brain damage in a circumscribed area and impaired performance on a particular test. I argued at the beginning of this chapter that to seek mere associations is dangerous because it so frequently leads to false-positive results. I also argued that merely saying that there is a link between brain damage and test performance provides an inadequate account at both the physiological and the psychological level. We need to know, first, the effects of the brain damage on overall brain function, and, second, the nature of the cognitive processes underlying test performance.

Any psychological test involves many cognitive processes, only some of which will be relevant to localisation. We might call these processes "specific" and "non-specific". If impairment is restricted to a very small range of tests, then it is more plausible that a specific process is impaired. This is because the non-specific processes will be shared by many tests. Thus, if the patient's performance is adequate on most tests, then it is likely that non-specific processes underlying performance on most tests are intact. Conversely, a patient who is impaired on a wide range of tests, as is the case with many schizophrenic patients, is likely to have a deficit that affects non-specific processes.

Interpretation of the pattern of performance critically depends on analysing neuropsychological tests in terms of component cognitive processes. This, of course, is the programme of cognitive neuropsychology. Tim Shallice's book, *From neuropsychology to mental structure* (Shallice, 1988) provides many detailed examples in which test performance is analysed in this way. One of my principal aims in the rest of this book will be to demonstrate links between particular signs and symptoms of schizophrenia and test performance in terms of cognitive processes. Once we have understood signs and symptoms in this way, we have a chance of linking them with underlying brain dysfunction.

CHAPTER 4

Behavioural Abnormalities

NEGATIVE AND POSITIVE SIGNS

Most of the negative symptoms of schizophrenia are behavioural abnormalities and thus should more properly be called signs. I call them behavioural abnormalities because clinicians assess them by observing behaviour. Paradoxically these behavioural signs are more difficult to assess reliably than the subjective, positive symptoms. As a consequence there are many studies concerned with the definition and assessment of negative signs and with studying their natural history (when they develop and how they relate to outcome; see Lewine, 1985). Few studies have attempted to understand the cognitive processes which underlie negative signs (Table 4.1).

In the last chapter, I raised the possibility that negative features might be a secondary consequence of schizophrenia. A number of writers (e.g. Hemsley, 1977; Miller, 1960) have suggested that negative signs reflect a strategy adopted to cope with the cognitive abnormalities that give rise to positive symptoms. For example, if positive symptoms reflect an overloading of the mind with irrelevant perceptions (the defective filter hypothesis), then reduction of stimulation by withdrawal from complicated situations (especially social situations) should ameliorate positive symptoms. However, negative signs can be present in the early stages of the illness (Montague et al., 1989) or even before the first appearance of positive symptoms (Wing, 1976). Furthermore, the old

Table 4.1
Some of the behavioural abnormalities (signs)
associated with schizophrenia (from Wing et al., 1974)

A) Negative signs	
Poverty of speech	Answers are restricted to the minimum number of words necessary. There are no extra sentences or unprompted comments (see Example 4.1)
Flattening of affect	Face and voice are expressionless. The patient does not become involved with the interview or respond emotionally to changing topics
Retardation	The patient sits abnormally still, walks abnormally slowly, takes a long time to initiate movements
Social withdrawal	The patient actively withdraws and refuses company when it is offered
B) Positive signs	
Incoherence of speech	Grammar is distorted, there are unexpected shifts of topic, there is a lack of logical connection between sentences
Incongruity of affect	The emotion expressed is not in keeping with that expected. For example, the patient may laugh when discussing a sad event
Stereotypies	The patient performs certain repetitive movements, such as rocking to and fro on a chair, rubbing their head round and round with their hand, nodding their head or grimacing

Kraepelinian view that negative signs are primary and a necessary part of "true" schizophrenia has recently been gaining ground. Negative signs are more strongly associated with social decline and cognitive impairment than are positive symptoms (e.g. Frith et al., 1991b). Thus, it is strange to think of negative symptoms as a coping strategy, as this strategy is not helping the patient to function better. The strategy leads to greater impairments than are found in patients who show positive symptoms, but no negative features. Finally, negative signs are associated with various neurological signs, such as movement disorders, which are all strongly suggestive of a biological basis (Owens & Johnstone, 1980). Indeed there are studies showing that negative signs are associated with structural brain changes such as enlarged ventricles (e.g. Andreasen et al., 1982). All this evidence suggests that negative features are a primary feature of schizophrenia. It must be remembered, however, that these features can also be observed in other conditions, such as depression. In this chapter I shall consider the cognitive basis of these signs and also of the positive behavioural features: incoherence of speech and incongruity of affect.

Poverty of Action and Poverty of Speech

As the label implies, the negative signs of schizophrenia are concerned with lack of behaviour. This is true for many domains: poverty of action, thought, speech, emotion, and social interactions (see Table 1.3). A patient who shows a lack of activity in one domain is likely to show this in the other domains as well (see Table 1.5). It is not the case, however, that the patient cannot or will not do anything when asked; patients are usually compliant and will perform complex psychological tests and answer difficult questions. Poverty of action is most easily illustrated in terms of speech. In Example 4.1 I have transcribed the responses of a patient with marked poverty of speech who was taking part in a standard clinical interview.

This interview contrasts strikingly with that shown in Example 4.2. The second patient is on the same ward as the first and my example comes from the same standardised assessment. This patient has also been in hospital a very long time, but shows no sign of poverty of speech.

The lack of behaviour in patients with negative features seems to occur specifically in situations in which actions have to be self generated. In Example 4.1 the patient answered all questions, but never volunteered new information or spontaneously elaborated his answers. This observation leads to a prediction: patients with negative signs should perform well with tasks in which responses are largely specified by the experimenter. They should perform badly when there is no such specification, even if the actual responses required are the same. This should apply, not just to speech, but to any activity.

We have, in these observations, the beginnings of a cognitive model for behavioural signs. This model assumes that there are two major sources of action. Some actions are carried out directly in response to environmental stimuli. Others are seemingly spontaneous and self-initiated. The theory that I propose assumes that patients with behavioural features have a specific difficulty with the latter type of action (Frith, 1987). This problem will manifest itself in different ways depending on the kind of response that is acceptable in the circumstances. Figure 4.1 shows a diagram of these two routes to action. This model is based on a number of theoretical developments and empirical observations that were not directly concerned with explaining features of schizophrenia. The physiological studies of Passingham (1987) and Goldberg (1985) will be discussed at the end of this chapter. Another major source for the model was studies of reaction time in humans (e.g. Frith & Done, 1986).

We can examine the explanatory power of this model with the example of fluency tasks. These tasks require the subject to generate

Example 4.1 Poverty of speech

E   How're you doing generally at the moment, Mr D?

D   All right

E   You're OK. How're...How've you been feeling in your spirits this past week?

D   Not so bad.

E   You're feeling all right. Do you have any spells of feeling sad or miserable?

D   No

E   No? Nothing like that? That's good. Now tell me, Mr. D, do you have any special ideas about life in general?

D   [shakes head]

E   No? Just ordinary ideas just like the rest of us. No. Have you ever thought that you were a special person in any way?

D   [shakes head]

E   No. Do you feel people stare at you and talk about you in some way?

D   [shakes head]

E   No. No, you didn't get bothered with that at all. Do you feel in any way that people are against you and trying to do you harm?

D   [shakes head]

E   No. You didn't get that either. That's good. Now I'd like to ask you some questions about your thoughts, Mr. D. Do you ever feel that your thoughts or your actions are influenced in some way?

D   [minimal head shake]

E   You didn't get that. You didn't get that. That's fine. Now could I ask you a routine question that we ask everyone? Do you ever seem to hear voices or noises when you're alone and you're wide awake which other people don't hear?

D   [shakes head]

E   You don't get that.

D   [shakes head]

E   No? Do you not get any of those things at all? No. Do you feel unwell in any way at all?

D   [shakes head]

E   You feel fine?

D   [nods head]

E   Do you feel the same way as you felt before you took ill?

D   Mh

E   You do?

D   ...

E   Well that's good.

Example 4.2 Normal speech

E   Well, how've things been this past week for you? Quite OK?

H   Er. Not too bad.

E   Not any special problems?

H   Well...special problems?...Not really.

E   How've you been in your spirits this past week?

H   Well, it goes...it goes...If you drew a graph, it would go up and down a bit.

E   Up and down a bit.

H   It goes up at night usually.

E   You're a bit worse in the morning, a bit more miserable?

H   No. It's all right once I've had breakfast, you know, and a cigarette.

E   When you get going you're all right. Not any long spells of being miserable or anything like that?

H   No

E   No. OK. Have you been worrying a lot during the past month?

H   No, I don't worry. I usually...

E   You don't worry.

H   I generally write, you see. I write letters, you know.

E   Uh hu. Letters to friends and that sort of thing?

H   Not really. I write to New Scotland Yard at the moment.

---

responses with minimal specification by the experimenter, for instance "name as many animals as you can". With this verbal fluency task the subject must find, within a given time limit, a series of different words. The task is not to generate completely novel words, merely to find and say appropriate words that already exist in his mental lexicon. Typically, a patient with negative signs will produce extremely few words. However, there are other abnormalities that may be observed when someone who has difficulty in generating spontaneous responses is asked to produce words in a fluency task (Example 4.3).

These three types of abnormality can all be seen as consequences of the impairment in the "willed" route to action illustrated in Figure 4.1. What will happen if you can not generate a spontaneous new response? There are three possibilities. First, you might do nothing (poverty of action). Second, you might repeat your previous response, even though it is now inappropriate (perseverative, stereotyped responding). Third, you might respond inappropriately to some signal in the environment (stimulus-driven behaviour, or what Luria (1973) calls an inert stereotype). What sort of abnormality will emerge also depends on the nature of the task the subject is trying to perform. In the verbal fluency task the subject is explicitly told not to repeat words and most subjects

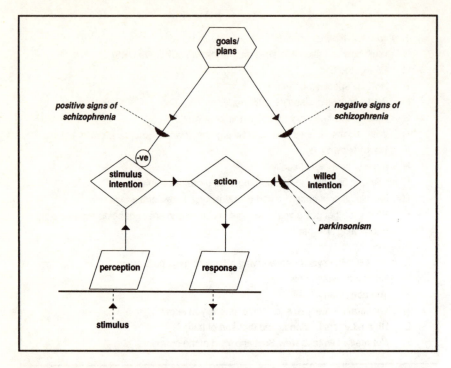

FIG. 4.1 Two routes to action. Stimulus-driven action: perception→stimulus intention→action→response; willed action: goals/plans→willed action→response. Three disconnections are shown: (1) goals fail to generate intentions: negative features (poverty of action); (2) goals fail to inhibit stimulus-driven actions (-ve indicates inhibiting effect.): positive features (incoherence of action); (3) willed intentions fail to generate actions: Parkinsonism.

can comply with this demand. As a consequence perseverative behaviour is rarely observed. In Example 4.3 patient K did not say "cheetah" all the time even though he could not stop thinking of it.

With another task, design fluency (make as many different designs as you can), the subject has to create many novel designs (Jones-Gotman & Milner, 1977). Typically, in this task patients with schizophrenia will produce many designs, but they are all remarkably similar (Kolb & Wishaw, 1983). Thus, difficulty in generating responses spontaneously can either result in few responses or in stereotyped responses depending on the kind of responses that are acceptable.

My model for poverty of action proposes that schizophrenic patients with negative signs have difficulty in generating actions spontaneously. On the basis of this model we would expect such patients not only to show a lack of action. In certain circumstances we would also expect

Example 4.3 Three types of abnormal verbal fluency
All the patients were asked to give all the animals they could think of in three minutes.

Patient F produced 4 words in three minutes
  goat
  calf
  lion
  puppy

Patient K produced 14 words, but had problems with perseveration
  lions
  tigers
  cheetahs
  all the animals in the zoo
  turtles
  cheetah
  can't think of any more
  whale
  the only one I can think of is cheetah
  lions
  lion
  lioness

Patient H produced 29 words, but many were not animals
  ...
  emu
  duck
  swan
  lake
  Loch Ness monster
  bacon
  bacon & eggs
  pig
  porky pig
  pig sty

them to show stereotyped behaviour or an excess of stimulus-driven behaviour. Thus the same underlying deficit can lead to different kinds of surface behaviour.

Unfortunately, the converse is also true. Different deficits can lead to the same surface behaviour. This dissociation between behaviour and the underlying causes of behaviour makes clear the danger of relying solely on objective behavioural observations. We can use again the example of verbal fluency. The verbal fluency task is one in which the subject has to generate responses with minimal help from external cues. The subject has to perform a self-directed search through their inner lexicon to find words that are members of the designated category. Schizophrenics with negative signs produce abnormally few items. The same behaviour is shown by patients with organic dementia, but for different reasons. Schizophrenics with negative symptoms produce few items because they find it difficult to perform a self-directed search. Demented subjects produce few items because the inner lexicon itself has become depleted and contains fewer words. Thus, however efficient the search, only few items will be found. In such cases performance on the verbal fluency task is predictable from the size of the vocabulary (Miller, 1984). Shallice (1988) has labelled these two defects impaired access and degraded store. Some depressed patients also show impaired verbal fluency. Presumably this is also due to a problem of impaired access rather than degraded store. It seems very reasonable that depressed patients should also have a problem with "willed" actions. However, in their case this may be secondary to the depression. They do not want to act, while the schizophrenic patient cannot want to act.

Stereotypies and Perseverations

Stereotyped behaviour is a prominent feature of schizophrenia and had been associated with madness long before the syndrome of schizophrenia was first described. Nehemia Grew wrote in 1701, "We see also Mad people, in whom Phancy reigns, to run upon some one action, as Reading, or Knitting of Straws, without variation." John Ferrier in 1795 described stereotyped communication very similar to that observed in schizophrenic patients today, "When lunatics attempt to write, there is a perpetual recurrence of one or two favourite ideas, intermixed with phrases which convey scarcely any meaning either separately, or in connection with the other parts. It would be a hard task for a man of common understanding, to put such rhapsodies into any intelligible form, yet patients will run their ideas in the very same track for many weeks together ..."

Surprisingly, stereotyped behaviour does not feature strongly in modern accounts of schizophrenia. For example, in the *Handbook of Psychiatry*, (Wing & Wing, 1982) Kraepelin's view of the importance of stereotyped behaviour in schizophrenia is quoted in the introduction, but the topic is never mentioned again. Furthermore, stereotyped behaviour is not usually included in instruments for assessing psychotic signs and symptoms (e.g. the Krawiecka scales). In contrast, stereotypies are reported widely in the animal literature and in the neurological literature (e.g. Cooper & Dourish, 1990).

John Done and I have found that it is possible to elicit stereotyped behaviour in schizophrenics using a two-choice guessing task (Frith & Done, 1983). In the earliest version of this task (Frith, 1970) a shuffled pack of playing cards was used. Subjects had to guess whether the next card would be red or black. In more recent versions a computer generates the random sequence and the subjects indicate their response by pressing buttons. In this task the subject has minimal external help in choosing the next response. Faced with such a problem, the normal subject produces a roughly random sequence of guesses similar to the sequence generated by the computer. We can define stereotyped behaviour in this situation as occurring when the current response made by a subject can be predicted from his previous responses. In practice only two kinds of predictable response sequence seem to occur; alternations (LRLRLRLR) and perseverations (LLLLLLLL). Alternations seem to be a less severe example of stereotyped behaviour than perseverations. There is a developmental trend in young children progressing from perseverations, through alternations to random performance (Gerjuoy & Winters, 1968). Likewise, perseverations are characteristic of chronic schizophrenic patients with negative signs and intellectual impairment, while alternations are seen in patients with negative signs at an earlier stage of the illness (Frith & Done, 1983; Lyon, Mejsholm, & Lyon, 1986).

Stereotyped behaviour can be much reduced by altering the way in which the task is perceived. This can be done by altering the nature of the event the subject is trying to guess. I devised a video game version of the task in which the subject has to dodge on-coming enemy space ships. The subject could either dodge to the left or the right. If the "correct" choice was made the enemy ship passed harmlessly by. If the "wrong" choice was made then there was a collision and an explosion. In this version of the task, the majority of subjects, whether normal or psychotic, were strongly influenced by the outcome of the previous trial. If there was a collision then the subject would dodge the other way on the next trial. If there was no collision he would dodge the same way. This "win-stay lose-shift" strategy was almost never observed in the earlier version of the task in which subjects had to guess in which box a cross would be hidden and where there was no striking consequence of making the wrong choice.

The space-ship dodging task was also much less likely to induce stereotyped behaviour in the schizophrenic patients. What is the explanation of this difference? In the space ship task, both normal and schizophrenic subjects used an external event to determine their responses. This event was the direction moved by the space ship on the preceding trial. Because they generated their responses in this way schizophrenic patients did not show alternation or repetition of responses. Instead they showed normal stimulus-elicited behaviour in which their response was determined by the immediately preceding event. Abnormalities of will are only observed when the action truly has to be self-generated, when no stimulus is available to determine the response.

Incoherence and Incongruity

Incoherence of speech and incongruity of affect are traditionally classified as positive symptoms because they are abnormal by their presence. However, in factor analytic studies of signs and symptoms (e.g. Liddle, 1987a) incoherence and incongruity formed a separate cluster from hallucinations and delusions. Incoherence and incongruity are clearly behavioural signs, so that, in my scheme, they should be classified with the negative features of schizophrenia. I propose that these signs reflect the third type of impairment that I have related to defects of willed action, that is, inappropriate responses elicited by stimuli. There is a long history of research suggesting that schizophrenic patients can be "captured" by immediate details of stimuli, even when the resultant response is inappropriate in the wider context (e.g. Salzinger et al., 1978). However, none of this work related the behaviour to specific signs and symptoms. Recently, Liddle and Morris (1991) found that incongruity and incoherence were associated with bad performance on the Stroop test (Perret, 1974). In this task subjects have to suppress the habitual tendency to read words by naming the colour of the ink when the word RED is written in blue. In our study of a large group of patients in the Harrow area (Frith et al., 1991b) we found that incoherence and incongruity were associated with a failure to inhibit inappropriate responses on the Continuous Performance Task. In this task subjects have to respond when they see the letter E on a screen, except when it is preceded by the letter X. Incoherent patients responded to E even when it was preceded by X. In addition, many of the features of incoherent language described by clinicians explicitly concern stimulus-elicited abnormalities. Examples from Andreasen's scale for assessing language disorders are: distractible speech (stopping during speech in response to a nearby stimulus), derailment (ideas slip off track, onto another that is nearly related), and clanging (sounds rather than meanings govern word choice). Patient H in Example 4.3 was failing to suppress inappropriate associations (e.g. swan–lake) when trying to generate animals in the verbal fluency task. I would conclude therefore that the positive abnormalities of behaviour observed in schizophrenia can also be explained in terms of a failure of willed action in which action is instead excessively determined by irrelevant stimuli. I have illustrated this in Figure 4.1 by showing a pathway that inhibits stimulus-driven acts if these are incompatible with current plans. This inhibition fails in some patients with schizophrenia.

Flattening of Affect and Social Withdrawal

If negative signs reflect a problem with spontaneous, self-initiated action, then signs such as poverty of will (lack of volition), poverty of speech, and poverty of thought start to become explicable. It is less clear how this formulation of the underlying cognitive deficit can explain the other major signs: social withdrawal and flattening of affect.

What aspect of behaviour is being by considered by a psychiatrist assessing "flattening of affect"? In the Present State Examination (Wing et al., 1974), flattening of affect is defined as follows: "The subject's face and voice are expressionless, he does not become involved in the interview or respond emotionally to changing topics of conversation ..." Psychiatrists assess "flattening of affect" from a clinical interview. In such a context strong, "real" emotions, which change rapidly are neither likely nor appropriate. What the psychiatrist will be observing are the rapidly fluctuating and often subtle shifts of expression that accompany all conversations. These changes in emotional expression play an important part in amplifying and facilitating communication. We laugh or make a sad face to indicate that we are being facetious or that we regret having to be critical. Even a stiff upper lip or a poker face can be put into the service of deliberately communicating an attitude (e.g. stoicism, mistrust). It is impairments in producing these subtle aspects of non-verbal communication that are rated as "flattening of affect". This sign is one of many in a larger domain that might be labelled "poverty of communication" (see Chapter 6). From this point of view "flattening of affect" could be relabelled "poverty of gesture". Such a sign can more readily be seen as another example of a lack of spontaneous, self-initiated action.

Few studies have investigated the cognitive basis of flattening of affect and social withdrawal directly. On the other hand, recognition of facial expression is clearly relevant to both these signs. There have been numerous experiments investigating the ability of schizophrenic patients to perceive faces and, in particular, to distinguish and label emotional expressions (see Cutting, 1985, pp. 294–297 for a review; also Gessler et al., 1989). These studies show that schizophrenics are poor at identifying emotional expressions and probably perceive faces in an abnormal way. Furthermore, Braun et al. (1991) have shown that schizophrenic patients have difficulty in using their faces to express emotion. Schizophrenic patients are also impaired in the use of the voice to express emotion (Murphy & Cutting, 1990). Leff and Abberton (1981) have related this problem directly to clinical ratings of flatness of affect. Patients with this sign had monotonous voices in terms of objective measures of frequency components. These results have obvious implications for the signs of social withdrawal and flattening of affect Difficulty in reading the emotions of others would make social interactions difficult. We might also speculate that if someone has difficulty in reading the emotions of others then they might also have difficulty in reading their own emotions. Of course, causation might be the other way round. Reduced social contact may also lead to poor ability to interpret faces and emotions.

The difficulty that many schizophrenic patients have with recognising emotions may be part of a larger problem with making inferences about mental states. Heidi Allen (1984) asked chronic patients to describe pictures involving people (TAT cards). It was striking that these patients, particularly those with speech problems (poverty, incoherence) hardly ever described what the people in the pictures were doing in terms of mental states. In contrast, controls would often use expressions of the type, "she's unhappy about something", "they're arguing with each other" and so on. A problem with inferring the contents of thoughts and feelings of others would make social interactions immensely difficult. Similar findings are reported by McPherson et al. (1970) and Bodlakova, Hemsley, & Mumford (1974). These workers used the "repertory grid" technique in which patients are asked to think of differences and similarities between pairs of people. Schizophrenic patients, particularly those with flattening of affect were significantly less likely to use "psychological" terms (e.g. kind) and more likely to use physical terms (e.g. tall).

In part, flattening of affect and social withdrawal may reflect a more basic poverty of action and communication that stems from a problem with the generation of spontaneous "willed" action. However, these features may also reflect problems that patients have in monitoring their own mental states and also those of others. I shall discuss these problems in more detail in Chapters 6 and 7.

I propose that the various behavioural abnormalities associated with schizophrenia are best understood in terms of a fundamental defect in the generation of willed action. This defect can result in three types of abnormality: (1) poverty of action, (including speech and thought); (2) perseverative or stereotyped action; and (3) inappropriate, stimulus-driven, action. Figure 4.1 illustrates how these abnormalities would follow from such a defect: (1) the patient fails to form willed intentions on the basis of current goals and so no willed actions are initiated; (2) the link between goals and actions is necessary, not only for the initiation of acts, but also for the termination of actions, as actions are normally terminated when the goal is achieved. Lack of this normal termination results in perseverative and stereotyped behaviour; (3) the same mechanism that initiates and terminates actions, also inhibits inappropriate stimulus driven actions. Lack of this inhibition leads to incoherent behaviour.

HOW DO THE BEHAVIOURAL ABNORMALITIES OF SCHIZOPHRENIA RELATE TO THE BRAIN?

There is a particular reason why it should be easier to answer this question for negative signs than for positive symptoms. Negative signs involve observable behaviour and it is possible to observe the same behaviour in animals. Thus "animal models" of schizophrenia have tended to be concerned with negative signs. In this section I shall consider evidence from lesion studies in animals and studies of neurological patients to see if the behavioural abnormalities observed in schizophrenia can be related to any particular brain locations.

Negative Features and Brain Lesions

"Psychomotor retardation" is a phenomenon, often observed in neurological patients, which has much in common with the negative features of schizophrenia. Benson (1990), for example, includes the following as features of psychomotor retardation; decreased activity level, social withdrawal, decreased interpersonal communication, flatness of vocal inflection, and unchanging facial expression. Among the most common causes of psychomotor retardation listed by Benson are frontal lobe damage and Parkinson's disease. Although patients with these different disorders have certain features in common, in the main their behaviour is very different. Clearly, negative features can occur in the context of very different disorders (including depression, for example) and are associated with damage in a number of different brain areas. I have illustrated these differences in Figure 4.1. In Parkinson's disease willed intentions are formed, but cannot be converted into actions: patients know what they want to do, but cannot do it. In contrast, patients with frontal lobe lesions are unable to form the appropriate sequence of intentions needed to achieve their goals. In this example, we see how the same surface behaviour may be the result of quite different cognitive abnormalities.

The specific areas of frontal cortex in which damage produces these behavioural changes have been listed by Damasio and Van Hoesen (1983). They conclude that the "limbic" frontal lobe is the principal system involved: orbito-frontal cortex, cingulate cortex, and supplementary motor area (SMA). Patients with damage in the cingulate cortex and/or SMA tend to become mute and show lack of spontaneous movement. Case J (Damasio & Van Hoesen, 1983) showed a striking contrast between her lack of spontaneous speech and her ability to repeat words and sentences. Electrical stimulation of the cingulate cortex can generate what I call "stimulus-driven" behaviour. "For instance, if a banana or an orange were shown, the patient would start eating it, often without appropriately peeling it. If (electrical) stimulation was interrupted the subject would ... abandon the task. Most subjects perceived the action as imposed from the 'exterior' " (Damasio & Van Hoesen, 1983). This phenomenon is strikingly similar to the "utilisation" behaviour described by Lhermitte (1983), which I shall discuss in a later section on stereotypies.

Passingham and his colleagues have conducted a series of elegant experiments on self-initiated actions in the monkey (see Passingham, Chen, & Thaler, 1989). The monkeys sit in a cage, and, whenever they want a peanut, they reach through the bars and raise an arm. There is no visible target and there is no change in the environment to tell the animals when to raise their arm. After lesions of the supplementary motor area (and after lesions of cingulate cortex) performance of these self-initiated actions is grossly impaired. In contrast, monkeys with SMA lesions can still perform tasks when there is a sound or a patch of colour indicting which action to make. Passingham concludes that the SMA lesion makes it difficult for the monkey to retrieve from memory the appropriate movement unless help is given by an external cue. These results show that there is neurophysiological justification for the distinction between the two routes to action that I have shown in Figure 4.1.

In humans, lesions restricted to the orbito-frontal cortex are very rarely seen. Damasio and Van Hoesen suggest that these lesions are associated with apathy, facetiousness, and impaired social judgement. Similar changes can be observed after experimental lesions of orbito-frontal cortex in monkeys. I shall discuss the brain lesions underlying social interactions more fully in Chapter 7.

Parkinson's Disease and Negative Features

Parkinson's disease relates to schizophrenia, not only because similar negative features can be observed in both disorders, but also because the neurotransmitter, dopamine, is implicated in both. The "dopamine hypothesis" of schizophrenia (Randrup & Munkvad, 1972) was based largely on two observations. First, that amelioration of symptoms by drugs depends upon blockade of the dopamine receptor (Seeman et al., 1976). Second, that amphetamine, which releases dopamine, can induce schizophrenic signs and symptoms (Connell, 1958). Thus the "dopamine hypothesis" was formulated; schizophrenia is associated with too much dopamine or, at least, an over-stimulated dopamine system. In this context, Parkinson's disease is of great interest because this disorder is known to be associated with a lack of dopamine in the striatum (see Appendices 4 & 5; Ehringer & Hornykiewicz, 1960). Thus we would expect that Parkinson's disease should, in some sense, be the opposite of schizophrenia. However, many of the negative signs of schizophrenia are also observed in Parkinson's disease. For example, the major problem in Parkinson's disease can be described as poverty of action (e.g. akinesia, bradykinesia).

As I have said before, we must be aware that the same sign can arise for a different reason. The patient with Parkinson's disease is prevented from acting by a difficulty at the stage of motor output. In contrast the patient with chronic schizophrenia probably has no action in mind to perform. Likewise, the patient with Parkinson's disease has "facial rigidity" while the patient with schizophrenia has "flattening of affect". Thus, in terms of surface behaviour, there are many similarities between Parkinson's disease and schizophrenia. Almost certainly, however, different cognitive impairments underlie this surface behaviour. It has also been suggested that patients with Parkinson's disease are impaired in willed action, but not stimulus-driven action (e.g. Goldberg, 1985). There are many anecdotes reporting that Parkinson patients can perform vigorous actions in certain special circumstances, while otherwise remaining "frozen". This phenomenon is known as "paradoxical kinesis" (Marsden et al., 1982). However, it has yet to be demonstrated that these unexpected actions have, in some sense, been elicited by external stimuli.

In conclusion, studies of negative features in neurological patients implicate several brain areas: prefrontal cortex (especially medial and lateral areas) and the striatum. These areas are modulated by the dopamine system.

Stereotypy and Perseveration in Neurological Patients

Luria suggests that patients with frontal lobe lesions show various kinds of stereotyped behaviour. This can take the form of repetitive, pointless or inappropriate responses. Having once produced an action, the patient will continue to produce that action even though it is no longer required. For example, Luria (1973, p. 207) reports of a patient with a massive injury to the left frontal region that, "Having once drawn a cross the patient continued to draw it even when instructed to draw a circle, and the patient having drawn a circle or a square continued to repeat this action whatever the task given". Luria also describes another kind of stereotyped behaviour, which he calls "inert stereotypy". In this case the patient makes standard responses to stimuli which are inappropriate in the current context, "One patient, for example, on seeing the button operating a bell, was involuntarily drawn to it and pressed it, and when the nurse came in response to the bell, he was unable to say why he had done so" (Luria, 1973, p. 200). I call this "stimulus-driven" behaviour. Luria's accounts are somewhat anecdotal, but subsequent, more carefully controlled studies have confirmed many of his observations (see Shallice, 1988). Lhermitte (1983), for example, has described "utilisation behaviour" in certain patients with frontal lesions. When such patients are handed a pair of spectacles they will put them on. However, handed another pair, they will put these on on top of the others. Showing the patient an object elicits a stereotyped (or stimulus-driven) response to that object even when such a response is inappropriate. The "alien hand" sign (Goldberg, Mayer, & Toglia, 1981) is probably a similar phenomenon associated with lesions of SMA. I shall discuss this sign in more detail in Chapter 5.

Shallice's Supervisory Attentional System (SAS)

At least three different behavioural abnormalities associated with schizophrenia seem to be observed in patients with frontal lesions: lack of self-initiated activity, perseverative and stereotyped activity, and inappropriate responses to stimuli. Shallice (1988) has explained all these kinds of behavioural abnormality in terms of defects in a "Supervisory Attentional System". Shallice is trying to explain how one of many different possible actions are selected and carried through to completion. (An action is a goal-directed response usually involving movement.) In the lower part of Figure 4.2 the many possible competing actions are illustrated. Each action can be triggered by an environmental stimulus. By a system of mutual inhibition, the most

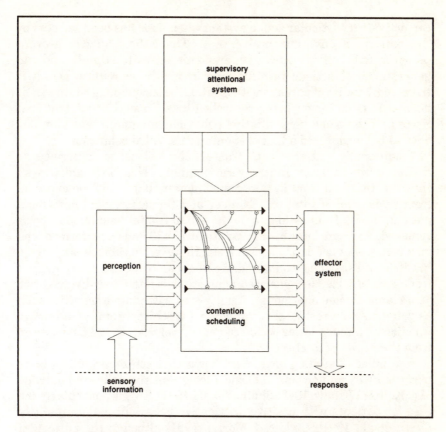

FIG. 4.2 Shallice's system for the control of action. In the contention scheduling system the different action schemas mutually inhibit one another. The supervisory attentional system modulates contention scheduling, inhibiting inappropriate routine actions and facilitating actions when none is specified by current sensory stimulation.

highly activated action "wins" and is carried through while the rest are temporarily suppressed. Shallice calls this process contention scheduling. On its own such a system is only capable of what I have called "stimulus-driven" behaviour. In the absence of environmental signals the system will do nothing or it will perseverate. However, this low level system can perform complex, routine actions perfectly well as long as they are sufficiently specified by the environment.

In Shallice's model, the contention scheduling mechanism is modulated from a higher level by a "Supervisory Attentional System" (SAS). The SAS can modify the strengths of the competing actions systems. For example, it might suppress the action currently most activated by environmental stimuli. By the same mechanism, the SAS can activate a particular action system when none has been selected by the pattern of environmental stimuli. Thus, the SAS can prevent perseverative behaviour, can suppress responses to stimuli, and can generate novel actions in situations in which no routine action is triggered. Studies of patients with frontal lobe lesions suggest that their behaviour is no longer being controlled by a Supervisory Attentional System. They show perseverative behaviour, inappropriate stimulus elicited behaviour and a lack of spontaneous willed behaviour.

Traditionally, patients with frontal lobe lesions are described as suffering from a defect in long-term planning. This is to explain why they function at a level in life so much lower than would be expected from their level of intellect. Eslinger and Damasio (1985) describe a patient, EVR, from whom a large orbito-frontal meningioma was removed. Six years later his IQ was still over 130 and he performed well on a wide variety of psychological tests. However, his ability to organise his life was disastrously impaired. He went bankrupt and was then fired from several jobs. He remarried against advice and was divorced two years later. He had enormous difficulty even with simple activities such as going out to a restaurant. Patients with schizophrenia also tend to function at a much lower socio-economic level than would be expected from their level of intellect.

A number of studies have also shown that schizophrenic patients perform badly on neuropsychological tests sensitive to frontal damage (e.g. Kolb & Wishaw, 1983; Shallice et al., 1991). This is particularly the case for patients with positive or negative behavioural abnormalities (Frith et al., 1991b; Liddle & Morris, 1991) although the pattern of abnormalities differs between these two subgroups: patients with negative signs tend to make errors of omission, while those with positive signs make errors of commission. However, much work still needs to be done to disentangle a specific "frontal" impairment from the general cognitive deficit seen in so many of these patients.

Stereotypies in Animals

Stereotyped behaviour has been extensively studied in animals. For example, it has been shown that amphetamine produces stereotyped behaviour in rats. This takes the form of repetitive, purposeless, and fragmented movements (see Robbins, 1982, for a review). In experiments in which the rat must respond in various ways to get rewards, amphetamine disrupts this responding, producing perseveration or response switching (e.g. Evenden & Robbins, 1983). Lyon and Robbins (1975) have proposed a general theory for this action of amphetamine. They suggest that, with increasing dose, there is an increased rate of response initiation with a reduction in the number of response categories. Nancy Lyon and her colleagues (Lyon et al., 1986; Lyon & Gerlach, 1988) have applied this theory to the behaviour of schizophrenics in the two-choice guessing task described earlier in this chapter. She has shown how, in terms of the Lyon–Robbins theory, an increasing severity in the underlying problem with response selection can lead first to response alternation and then to response perseveration. Trevor Robbins (1982) has related the Lyon—Robbins theory of stereotypy to Shallice's model for the selection of actions. He suggests that amphetamine acts to disrupt contention scheduling which is instantiated in the basal ganglia.

My own interpretation of the effects of amphetamine on contention scheduling goes as follows. In the normal situation an action is chosen on the basis of the pattern of activation induced by the current array of stimuli. The action most strongly activated occurs. Once an action has been selected, two inhibitory processes come into play. First, all other actions are temporarily inhibited. In psychological terms, the chosen action must be given a chance to prove its worth. Second, subsequent choice of the same action is temporarily inhibited. After the first action has had its turn other actions must be given a chance. Amphetamine interferes with both these temporary modulations of the action selection system. As a consequence the first action initiated is given less time to prove its worth before other actions are initiated. This results in an increased rate of action switching. At higher doses this switching occurs at a higher rate, but in addition the first action selected is no longer inhibited next time. As a consequence the same action is repeatedly initiated. In other words the stimulus array repeatedly elicits the same action with no short term modulation of selection consequent on the outcome of the action.

Studies of the rat tend to restrict interpretation to the level of the response. Ros Ridley and Harry Baker have carried out a series of studies on the effects of amphetamine in the marmoset (a small primate). In these studies they were able to use more sophisticated tasks and were therefore able to interpret the results in terms of cognitive processes (Ridley & Baker, 1983). Amphetamine induced stereotyped behaviour in these monkeys and also social withdrawal. Of particular interest was the observation that, in doses too small to elicit observable changes in spontaneous behaviour, amphetamine affected the performance of learning tasks. For example, the monkey has to learn that that there is always food in the well under a toy ballerina, but never under a toy soldier. Once this has been learned, the situation is reversed so that the soldier is rewarded. Under amphetamine the monkey learns the first part of the task normally, but takes much longer to reverse. This is because the monkey continues to approach the ballerina in a perseverative manner, even though this behaviour is no longer rewarded. Detailed investigation of this phenomenon showed that this was a cognitive perseveration. Once an object had acquired a positive connotation, then, under amphetamine, the monkey had great difficulty in learning to stop approaching that object. Similarly, if the monkey had learned to avoid an object then this avoidance would persist abnormally under amphetamine. Ridley and Baker conclude, "Two mechanism are involved in reversal learning, one actively inhibiting an inappropriate reward association and the other acquiring the new association … after amphetamine, it is the inhibitory system that is impaired or overriden". Ridley and Baker (1983, p. 125) note that the effects they observed after treatment with amphetamine are very similar to the effects of frontal lobe lesions on monkeys.

Subsequently Ridley and Baker looked at the effects of amphetamine on the same two-choice guessing task used by Frith and Done (1983) with schizophrenic patients. When given an inactive substance (saline) the monkeys made random sequences of responses like normal people. Under amphetamine they made very stereotyped sequences, like schizophrenic patients with negative signs (Ridley et al., 1988).

These studies of the effects of amphetamine in monkeys suggest that there are effects on selection for actions at the cognitive level that are very similar to the effects on rats at the level of simple responses. I interpret these results as showing that amphetamine alters the balance of response selection in favour of responses being largely "stimulus-driven" with little effect of the outcome of recent responses on the current activating properties of stimuli. In addition, amphetamine increases the general level of activity.

On this account, the effects of amphetamine should be most relevant for explaining the positive behavioural abnormalities of schizophrenia: incoherence and incongruity as well as stereotyped behaviour. However, there is a major problem with my attempt to link the effects of amphetamine on animals with the behavioural features of schizophrenia. In animals, amphetamine produces stereotyped behaviour. Such behaviour also occurs in schizophrenic patients with negative behavioural features. However, the amphetamine psychosis in man is associated with positive symptoms, especially delusions of persecution and auditory hallucinations (Connell, 1958). This difference between the effects of amphetamine in animals and man may be apparent rather than real. The rat and the monkey may be developing persecutory ideas, but we cannot know whether this is the case. Also, people taking large amounts of amphetamine develop stereotyped behaviour, but will not be labelled psychotic until they also develop positive symptoms. However, even if we can eliminate the differences in the effects of amphetamine on man and animal, I must allow that amphetamine effects are relevant for positive symptoms as well as behavioural signs. As Ridley and Baker (1983) point out, the failure of the monkey treated with amphetamine to abandon its false belief that there is food under the ballerina may resemble the failure of paranoid patients to abandon their false belief that people are persecuting them. In Chapter 5 I shall suggest how defects in the control of action might also give rise to positive symptoms.

BRAIN SYSTEMS UNDERLYING THE SELECTION OF ACTION

In this chapter I have suggested that the behavioural abnormalities of schizophrenia: poverty of action, stereotyped action, and incoherent action are the consequence of defects in the mechanisms underlying the generation of "willed" actions while the mechanisms underlying "stimulus-driven" actions remain largely intact. Gary Goldberg (1985) has reviewed the evidence for a physiological basis for these two routes to action (see also Passingham, 1987). He suggests that there is a medial system for willed actions and a lateral system for stimulus-elicited actions. The main structures specifically concerned with willed actions are the dorsolateral prefrontal cortex, anterior cingulate cortex, supplementary motor area, and basal ganglia. As we have seen, most of these regions are also implicated in studies in which behavioural abnormalities, similar to those observed in schizophrenic patients, have been observed in neurological patients and in animals. Trevor Robbins (1990) has reviewed the case for a frontostriatal dysfunction in schizophrenia. He comes down in favour of such a hypothesis, but concludes that the pathophysiological basis of schizophrenia is unlikely to be found in a single area such as the frontal lobe. Schizophrenia is more likely to be associated with altered functioning in a corticostriatal functional loop. Five such loops have been described by Alexander, DeLong, and Strick (1986). Robbins points out that all of these loops involve frontal regions as a target area and all are influenced by dopaminergic inputs to the striatum. I conclude that the behavioural abnormalities associated with schizophrenia, both positive and negative, are likely to reflect defects in a loop of this type involving both the frontal cortex and the striatum. In Figure 4.3 I have combined the "routes to action" model shown in Figure 4.1, the cognitive mechanisms proposed by Shallice (Figure 4.2), and the brain regions implicated in the last part of this chapter.

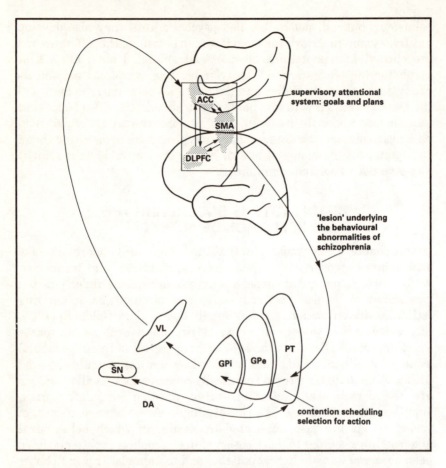

FIG. 4.3 Fronto-striatal loop (after Alexander et al., 1986) underlying the control of action. Abbreviations: ACC, anterior cingulate cortex; DA, dopamine; DLPFC, dorsolateral prefrontal cortex; GP, globus pallidus; PT, putamen; SMA, supplementary motor area; SN, substantia nigra; VL, ventrolateral nucleus of the thalamus.

Cools et al. (1984) have described, in much greater detail, a similar mapping between brain regions and mechanisms of motor control. Obviously this mapping must be very tentative, but it provides a useful framework for further research on the physiological basis of the behavioural abnormalities associated with schizophrenia.

Presumably abnormalities in different parts of the brain system associated with willed action may lead to the same surface abnormality such as poverty of action. However, the underlying cause will be different. Damage to prefrontal cortex will lead to a failure to develop the appropriate plan for action. At the other extreme, damage to the basal ganglia will not impair the patient's ability to form a plan of action, nor to select the appropriate response (at the level of intention). However, the patient will not be able to execute the response. The impairments associated with the abnormal behavioural features of schizophrenia lie, I believe, somewhere between these two extremes. At the cognitive level, this means that the patient may have a plan or a goal, but is unable to turn this into an appropriate action. At the physiological level, this means that there are disconnections between the prefrontal cortex and subcortical regions concerned with the control of action.

CHAPTER 5

Positive Symptoms, Abnormal Experiences

In Table 1.2 I listed the major positive symptoms associated with schizophrenia. These all concern abnormal experiences which the patient describes as best he can. Example 5.1 indicates how some of these experiences are typically labelled. By their nature, psychotic experiences are so unusual that patients find them very difficult to describe. For example, Patricia Ruocchio (1991) in her first person account, says, "There are things that happened to me that I have never found words for, some lost now, some which I still search desperately to explain ...". It is therefore necessary to be very cautious in interpreting these descriptions in terms of underlying cognitive abnormalities.

Karl Jaspers (1962, pp. 577–582) suggested that the characteristic feature of psychotic symptoms (by which essentially he meant positive symptoms) is that they are entirely outside the normal range of experiences. They are therefore impossible to "understand". He contrasts this with other kinds of symptom, like depression and anxiety, which are exaggerated forms of states we have all experienced. The schizophrenic patient describes something entirely outside the previously normal range of experience. Different people may well describe the same experience in different ways. We can all be easily misled as to the nature of our inner experiences and their most critical features. This applies even more so in the case of totally novel experiences. For example, "hearing my thoughts spoken aloud" and "believing that other people can read my thoughts" could be different

65

Example 5.1 Some psychotic experiences and the associated symptom label (from Leff, 1982 and Cutting, 1990)

a) I hear a voice saying, "You're not going to smoke the cigarette the way you want to." — Second person auditory hallucination

b) I hear a voice saying, "He is an astronomy fanatic. Here's a taste of his own medicine. He's getting up now. He's going to wash. It's about time." — Third person auditory hallucination

c) It was like my ears being blocked up and my thoughts shouted out. — Thought broadcast

d) Thoughts are put into my mind like "Kill God". It's just like my mind working, but it isn't. They come from this chap, Chris. They're his thoughts. — Thought insertion

e) The force moved my lips. I began to speak. The words were made for me. — Delusions of control

f) I saw someone scratching his chin which meant that I needed a shave. — Delusions of reference

g) People at work are victimising me. A bloke at work is trying to kill me with some kind of hypnosis. — Delusions of persecution

---

descriptions of the same experience. This difficulty in inferring the patient's experience from their description of it renders any attempt to classify positive symptoms problematic. Traditionally, positive symptoms have been divided into hallucinations (Example 5.1 a, b, & c) and delusions (Example 5.1 d, e, f, & g). This division is based on the belief that hallucinations are false perceptions while delusions are false beliefs. By the end of this chapter I hope I shall have convinced the reader that this distinction is not justified.

How one understands and classifies positive symptoms depends on one's hypotheses about the processes that underlie these symptoms. One theory of delusions is that they are the result of attempting to understand abnormal experiences by the application of normal reasoning processes (e.g. Maher, 1974). On such a theory delusions would be seen as understandable secondary responses to the primary abnormal experience of hallucinations. Others (e.g. Bentall, Kaney, & Dewey, 1991b) have suggested that it is the reasoning processes leading to delusions that are abnormal. In this case the delusions are the primary problem. As with the different diagnostic systems, endless fun can be had devising schemes for classifying positive symptoms and deciding which are primary and which secondary. These schemes are all arbitrary unless they can be shown to relate to some other level of description, such as cognitive mechanisms or physiology. One of my primary aims in writing this book is to show that consideration of the cognitive basis of the experiences of schizophrenic patients can provide a rational classification scheme for signs and symptoms that can be tested experimentally.

There is a major advantage of trying to explain positive symptoms in terms of underlying cognitive deficits. These deficits will give rise, not only to the positive symptoms, but also to peculiarities of behaviour. Such peculiarities may never have been reported clinically because they could be observed only in special situations. This is an advantage because it allows us to break out of circularity. We can make specific predictions about as yet unobserved behaviour, and then devise an experimental situation that probes this behaviour.

From a specific cognitive theory, we can predict that patients with positive symptoms will perform certain tasks in an abnormal way. This sort of hypothesis testing provides external validation for our classification of symptoms. If successful, the procedure will also yield objective measures, which will complement the subjective accounts of the patients. Patients grouped in terms of specific cognitive deficits should also share abnormalities at the physiological level. Such groupings would considerably enhance the likelihood for success in the search for the biological basis of schizophrenia.

Many have speculated about the psychological processes underlying positive symptoms such as hallucinations and delusions. However, there have been relatively few attempts to examine these hypotheses systematically by studying patients who have particular symptoms and contrasting them with patients who do not. All too often the hypotheses have been tested by contrasting "schizophrenics" with haphazardly defined control groups. Inevitably, the results have been uninformative. One of the most honourable exceptions to this rule is Peter Slade, who has been studying hallucinations in schizophrenic patients experimentally since the late 1960s. This has culminated in a book on hallucinations (Slade & Bentall, 1988) from which I shall draw frequently in this chapter.

HALLUCINATIONS

Hallucinations are usually defined as perceptions that occur in the absence of any appropriate stimulus. Typical schizophrenic hallucinations are restricted because, in most cases, these involve hearing the human voice. Only about 20% of schizophrenic patients report hallucinations in other modalities such as vision, touch or internal sensations. When the hallucinations first appear, the patient is quite convinced of the external reality of these experiences and may seek help in finding out who is transmitting the messages and how this is achieved. This absolute belief in the reality of the voices is strikingly illustrated in Evelyn Waugh's novel *The ordeal of Gilbert Pinfold*, which I shall quote from in the section on delusions. In the later stages of the illness the patient will learn that the "voices" are not real. Nevertheless, the experiences still have the quality of "real" perceptions.

At one time it was believed that hallucinations could be induced in normal people by prolonged sensory deprivation. However, in a review of a large number of these studies Zuckerman (1969) found that only about 15% of the volunteers reported complex auditory experiences and few of these resembled schizophrenic hallucinations. In this section I shall be concerned only with the hallucinatory experiences of schizophrenic patients.

In a number of studies, Slade and his colleagues, have shown that the hallucinations of schizophrenic patients—this usually means the hearing of voices—can be altered by giving the patients something to listen to (e.g. Margo, Hemsley, & Slade, 1981). Listening to a series of simple tones to which the patient had to respond reduced the volume and frequency of hallucinations; listening to random noise had the opposite effect. This is an important result. It shows that hallucinations can, to some extent, be brought under experimental control. However, this result does not enable us to distinguish between the two major theories of hallucinations that I shall now consider. These are essentially "input" and "output" theories respectively.

Input Theories of Hallucinations

In their most concrete form, input theories of hallucinations state that a hallucination occurs when an external stimulus is misperceived. Something like this is described by the patient in the case of "functional" hallucinations. This is a rare symptom when the patient may say "When the door slams I hear the words, 'get out'". Input theories of hallucinations place the abnormality within those cognitive processes that underlie perception. On this basis a schizophrenic hallucination is like the experience of an anxious mother who thinks she hears her baby crying whenever she hears some unusual sound. There is much experimental work on this type of misperception (e.g. Warren, 1970) and we can therefore make predictions about how the underlying cognitive abnormality could be made manifest experimentally.

A stimulus is most likely to be misperceived when it is complex and ambiguous and when the signal to noise ratio is low (i.e. when the target sound is relatively weak and the surrounding irrelevant noise is relatively loud). The results of Slade and his colleagues fit in well with this prediction. Hallucinations are minimised by simple unambiguous auditory stimuli and maximised by random noise. Thus hallucinations are more likely to occur in situations in which we would expect misperceptions. The obvious question to ask is, "Do hallucinating patients have a tendency to misperceive stimuli?".

The sort of misperception we are talking about requires that when the subject is presented with stimulus A (running bath water), she perceives stimulus B (a baby crying). There are two ways in which such a misperception could occur.

Failure of Discrimination
One possibility is that the two stimuli (e.g. running water and a baby crying) appear more similar to the patient than to other people and are thus more likely to be confused. In the terms of signal detection theory, this is a problem with discrimination. We assume that, for two stimuli to be more difficult to discriminate, the noise associated with them must be increased. Thus, in noisy environments, misperceptions are more likely to occur. Some patients indeed report that hallucinations are more likely in such environments. However, most people are not induced to hallucinate in noisy environments, and schizophrenic patients can hallucinate even in quiet situations. Thus, if hallucinations are due to discrimination problems, then the abnormal noise would have to reside in the nervous system of the patient rather than in the environment. Collicutt and Hemsley (1981) used psychophysical methods to estimate the amount of internal noise when subjects had to discriminate between tones of different loudness. They found no evidence for an increase in internal noise in patients experiencing hallucinations. However, it is possible that there might be an increase in internal noise specifically associated with speech-like stimuli, rather than tones.

Abnormal Bias
A more likely cause of the misperceptions that might underlie hallucinations is a change in "bias". Any stimulus, particularly if it is noisy or ambiguous, has many possible interpretations. Which

interpretation we perceive depends not only on our ability to discriminate, but also on our bias. The anxious mother considers it of crucial importance to know if her baby is crying when she knows the baby is ill. The worst error she could make would be to fail to notice the crying. Consequently she may perceive many irrelevant sounds as crying. This bias towards the perception of crying is quite independent of her ability to discriminate.

The idea that schizophrenic hallucinations are due to some disorder of bias, is very plausible. Hallucinations tend to reflect the expectations and preoccupations of the patient. For example, Connie Cahill (personal communication) conducted a long interview with a hallucinating patient. Towards the end of the interview the voice was reported to be saying things like, "She's written enough, now" and "She has to go back to work". If hallucinations really are misperceptions, then it is striking that patients only misperceive noise as voices (since they hear voices when no voices are present) and never misperceive voices as noise. This seems more like a problem of one-sided bias than one of discrimination. Richard Bentall and Peter Slade have studied bias in schizophrenic patients with and without hallucinations (Bentall & Slade, 1985). Subjects heard a long sequence of auditory stimuli, in half of which (signal trials) the word "who" was present in a background of noise, while in the other half (noise trials) only the noise was presented. Hallucinating patients frequently claimed to hear the word "who" in the noise trials as well as in the signal trials. This reflects an abnormal bias towards hearing words when none are there.

John Done and I (in preparation) have also studied bias in schizophrenic patients. We argued that the bias must be towards perceiving sounds as words and that this should be most marked when the sounds were most word-like. We therefore used a lexical decision task. The subject had to decide whether or not the noise presented was a word. We used a computer to generate phoneme strings; some of these were words, some were word-like (but not actual words) and some were random phoneme strings. We found no evidence that patients with schizophrenia had a bias to perceiving words. In particular, we found no evidence that patients with hallucinations had such a bias. It is still possible, however, that patients with auditory hallucinations have a bias to hear noises as speech sounds even if they do not have a bias to hearing speech sounds as words.

I conclude that the direct evidence for hallucinations as the misperception of external stimuli is weak. If hallucinating schizophrenic patients perceive words abnormally, as this theory implies, then they should also show receptive language problems. In Chapter 6, I shall review evidence that suggests that their language problems are almost entirely expressive. In addition, a perceptual input theory of auditory hallucinations has always had difficulty in explaining some of the more specific hallucinations that seem to be characteristic of schizophrenia: hearing one's own thoughts, hearing people talking about you. Many of these phenomena are much better handled by the other major theory of hallucinations: output theory.

Output Theories

At its crudest, an output theory of hallucinations says that the patient is talking to himself, but perceives the voices as coming from somewhere else. We can examine this crude version of the theory very directly.

Is There Speech During Hallucinations?

Kandinskii (1890) was the first to suggest that there was a relationship between hallucinations and inner speech. Subsequently, Gould (1949) investigated a schizophrenic patient who heard voices almost continuously. This patient was observed to make frequent sounds from her nose and mouth. When this subvocal activity was amplified with a microphone it was found to be whispered speech which was qualitatively different from the patient's voluntary whispers. On the basis of the content of this speech and the patient's reports, Gould concluded that the subvocal speech corresponded to the "voices". For example, "... subvocal speech continued 'She knows. She's the most wicked thing in the whole wide world. The only voice I hear is hers. She knows everything. She knows all about aviation.' At this point the patient stated audibly: 'I heard them say I have a knowledge of aviation' ".

McGuigan (1966) followed up Gould's observation by measuring muscle action potentials in tongue and chin in ten hallucinating patients. However, only one of these patients was sufficiently cooperative to report exactly when his hallucinations were occurring. McGuigan found a significant increase in oral muscle activity just before this patient indicated hearing the voice.

Green and Preston (1981) replicated Gould's result in another patient. Like Gould they were able to record the patient's voice using a throat microphone. In this patient also the whispered voice was qualitatively different from the patient's normal voice. Furthermore, what this voice said corresponded to the report given by the patient of her hallucinations. Surprisingly there are no other reports in the literature of any attempts to follow up these studies. A systematic investigation of chronic patients using telemetric recording would be very valuable. First, to discover how frequently this phenomenon is found, and, second, to acquire detailed information about the content of hallucinations.

If hallucinations are the consequence of subvocal speech, then it should be possible to suppress them by occupying the speech musculature in some way. Bick and Kinsbourne (1987) found that holding the mouth wide open reduced auditory hallucinations in 14 out of 18 schizophrenic patients, while other manoeuvres such as making a fist had no effect. In a subsequent study of 17 patients, Green and Kinsbourne (1989) failed to replicate this result, but did find that humming significantly reduced the time spent hallucinating.

Hallucinations and the Articulatory Loop
It is, of course, possible for subvocal speech to occur in the absence of any detectable sound or muscle activity. Alan Baddeley and his colleagues (Baddeley, 1986) have investigated in some detail (in normal people) the role of an "articulatory loop" in working memory. Amongst other things this loop is used for the temporary storage of verbal material and to hold the "inner speech" needed for short-term memory tasks, such as remembering a telephone number. Baddeley concludes that "... the loop and its rehearsal processes are operating at a much deeper level ... apparently relying on central speech control codes which appear to be able to function in the absence of peripheral feedback ... It is not surprising that attempts to study inner speech through the monitoring of the peripheral speech musculature have had only limited success" (Baddeley, 1986). However, inner speech of this sort can still be studied objectively.

Tasks such as remembering a string of digits for a short time can be achieved by repeatedly saying the digits subvocally. This subvocal repetition is considered to use the "articulatory loop", which is a component of working memory. We can impair the function of this loop by asking subjects to say "blah blah blah" while trying to perform some task. This "articulatory suppression" impairs memory for visually presented strings of digits. Baddeley and Lewis (1981) suggest that phonological coding of visually presented material depends on two processes: the inner voice and the inner ear. The inner voice is the articulatory loop requiring subvocal speech. The inner ear holds some form of acoustic image. The inner voice is necessary for memory span tasks requiring phonological coding, while the inner ear is sufficient for making rhyme judgments about visually presented words, a task in which there is no memory component (Baddeley, 1986, p. 85). If hallucinations are the consequence of abnormalities in central speech processes (the inner voice and/or the inner ear), then we would predict that hallucinations should interfere with tasks involving phonological coding (and vice versa). Thus we would predict that the presence of hallucinations should interfere with digit span, but not non-verbal span tasks. In the previous section I presented evidence that hallucinations involve the inner voice and not the inner ear. In this case the presence of hallucinations should not interfere with the ability to make rhyme judgments. As far as I am aware, these studies have not yet been carried out.

Hallucinations in schizophrenic patients who are congenitally deaf are of particular interest. If hallucinations are false percepts, then it would seem unlikely that a person who has never heard anything could experience auditory hallucinations. Nevertheless there are reports of prelingually deaf people with schizophrenia insisting that they hear "voices" (e.g. Critchley et al., 1981). In this study ten out of twelve patients described "auditory" hallucinations. One patient (case 4) said that "he could see the arms and hands of the person signing to him". However, the other patients were unable to explain how they "heard" the voices. Nevertheless, they insisted that it was "hearing". For example, in case 2: "When pressed she insisted that she heard (finger spelling the word "heard") not lip-read". These accounts are not so problematic if auditory hallucinations are based on inner speech, rather than hearing. Prelingually deaf people usually have some speech, even though it may be poor and difficult to understand. Thus, as in hearing patients, the auditory hallucinations of the deaf can be based on inner speech. Another possibility, which I shall return to later, is that the experience of an auditory hallucination is something much more abstract than hearing voices. Rather, it might be "receiving meaningful information" (Basilier, 1973) or, perhaps, an experience of receiving a communication without any sensory component. Such an experience might be described as "hearing voices" or, as in the case of one deaf patient, seeing people signing.

Self-monitoring

I will now introduce a concept that is very central to my own account of positive symptoms: self-monitoring. If hallucinations are caused by inner speech, then the problem is not that inner speech is occurring, but that patients must be failing to recognise that this activity is self-initiated. The patients misattribute self-generated actions to an external agent. I have called this a defect of "self-monitoring" (Frith, 1987) because the patients are failing to monitor their own actions. There are a number of other positive symptoms of schizophrenia that explicitly concern the attribution of the patient's own actions to outside agents. These are the so-called "passivity experiences': thought insertion (Example 5.1 d), and delusions of control (Example 5.1 e). In Schneider's (1959) list of "first rank" symptoms these are defined as "made feelings, made impulses and made acts" in which a patient's own feelings, wishes or acts seem to be alien and under external control. Because these symptoms are all classified as delusions I shall discuss their cognitive basis in more detail in the next section. However, I consider that the cognitive basis of auditory hallucinations is essentially the same as that of these delusions and is due to a defect in a central monitoring system. One form of self-monitoring has been labelled "corollary discharge" (Sperry, 1950) or "re-afference copy" (von Holst & Mittelstaedt, 1950) and has been extensively studied by physiologists (see Gallistel, 1980). The importance of this mechanism is particularly apparent with eye movements.

Long ago, Helmholtz (1866) pointed out that each time we move our eyes, our image of the world moves across the retina. Yet the world stays still. Thus we are able to distinguish between movement on the retina due to movements in the world and movements on the retina due to our own movements. In order to achieve this, a "corollary discharge" is sent to some monitor system at the same time as a message is sent to the eye muscles. On the basis of this message, movement of the image on the retina is expected. Compensation occurs and the image is perceived as stationary. Thus, a distinction is made between movements of images due to our own eye movements and movements that are independent of us. This distinction is achieved by monitoring intentions to make eye movements.

This mechanism depends upon a comparison between intentions to move and actual movements. Misleading discrepancies can be introduced into the system in at least two ways. Helmholtz observed that, if we move our eye by poking it with our finger, the image of the world appears to jerk. In this case no message has arrived indicating an intention to use the eye muscles. The opposite kind of disruption can be achieved by partially paralysing the eye muscles with curare (Brindley & Merton, 1960). In this case a message is sent indicating an intention to move the eyes, but the expected movement does not occur. The world appears to move in the direction in which the movement would have occurred. In this example of eye movements, "feed forward" of intentions is used to distinguish between events due to our own actions and independent events in the outside world. This mechanism (corollary discharge) applies to limb movements as well as eye movements and presumably to our own speech as well. There are, therefore, very good reasons for believing that a form of self-monitoring plays a vital role in modifying our perception of the world. A number of authors have suggested that defects in some sort of self-monitoring process might lead to the experience of hallucinations.

Self-monitoring and Incoherence

Ralph Hoffman (1986) suggested that there is a link between incoherent speech and hallucinations. Hoffman proposes that schizophrenic speech appears incoherent because words and phrases that are unrelated to the theme of the conversation are inserted randomly into the patient's speech (see Chapter 6). Because these words are unrelated to what the patient intended to talk about they are perceived as alien, even though they stem from the patient. It is these "alien" phrases that are the basis of auditory hallucinations. Direct empirical support for this theory is lacking because, in most studies (e.g. Liddle, 1987a) no associations are found between hallucinations and incoherence of speech. A patient with auditory hallucinations is neither more nor less likely to be incoherent than any other patient.

Hoffman suggests that the patient's own acts are perceived as alien because they are unintended. He also links the mechanisms underlying positive behavioural disorders (see Chapter 4) with positive symptoms. The difference between hallucinations and incoherence might be along a continuum of severity. At the lower level of severity inappropriate words and phrases remain as inner speech and thought and are experienced as verbal hallucinations. At a higher level of severity these words and phrases are actually spoken and become mixed up with vocal speech. It is possible that, once the unintended speech becomes audible, then peripheral feedback from speech musculature ensures that patients recognise that it is their own speech.

Self-monitoring and Memory for Action

Self-monitoring of speech can be studied directly by asking people to remember whether they said something or not. Richard Bentall and his colleagues (Bentall et al., 1991a) asked patients either to generate category items (a fruit beginning with T) or to read out category items (a country—Norway). A week later they were asked to identify the source of these items and some similar new items. Thus for each item (e.g. tomato, Norway, tiger) they had to decide whether they had generated it (tomato), whether it had been given (Norway), or whether it was new (tiger). It was predicted that hallucinating patients would have difficulty distinguishing what they had generated from what had been provided by the experimenter. Psychotic patients were worse than normal volunteers at this task, whether or not they had hallucinations. Hallucinating patients were slightly more likely to misattribute to the experimenter, items they had generated themselves.

I have carried out a very similar experiment as part of a survey of all the schizophrenic patients in the Harrow area (Frith et al., 1991b). Patients were asked to generate category items (e.g. animals) and then listened while the experimenter read out more items in the same category. Ten minutes later the patient was asked to decide whether items were self-generated, experimenter-generated or new. Contrary to expectation, it was the incoherent and incongruous patients who were poor at distinguishing self-generated and experimenter-generated items, while this ability was unrelated to the presence of hallucinations.

Incoherent patients perform poorly on this task because it involves source memory as well as self-monitoring. I have suggested that incoherent patients behave in many ways like patients with frontal lobe lesions (Chapter 4). Source memory is impaired in patients with frontal lobe lesions (e.g. Janowsky et al., 1989), but this is because the patient cannot remember the external source of the material.

In order to use the methodology described by Bentall et al. (1991a) and Frith et al. (1991b) for the study of self-monitoring as distinct from source memory, it will be necessary to contrast two different source memory tasks. In one task subjects have to distinguish between two external sources, while in the other they must distinguish between an internal and an external source. Hallucinating patients should be impaired on the latter task relative to the former.

Harvey (1985) has used precisely this design, but he was studying thought disorder rather than hallucinations. In one task two experimenters alternately read out a series of words. Subjects had to remember which experimenter had said each word. This task requires memory for two external sources. In the second task subjects had to read out a series of words or to imagine themselves saying another series of words. Subsequently they had to remember which words had been thought and which spoken.

Harvey found that thought-disordered schizophrenic patients had more difficulty in discriminating what they had thought from what they had said in comparison to other psychotic patients and normal people. These patients were not impaired in distinguishing the two external sources in task 1. Unfortunately, Harvey did not investigate whether performance on his tasks was related to hallucinations. These results suggest that at least some schizophrenic patients do have impairments in monitoring their own speech. However, it remains to be seen if this is only true for patients who show predominantly the signs of thought disorder and incoherence, or whether it also applies to those showing auditory hallucinations

As yet there is no direct evidence that hallucinating patients have a specific problem with monitoring their own speech, as the critical experiments remain to be done. Nevertheless, I shall assume provisionally that at least some auditory hallucinations are based on inner speech which the patient misattributes to an external source.

It is unlikely that all hallucinations in schizophrenia are based on inner speech. The basic experience underlying many of the so-called "auditory" hallucinations is occurring at a more abstract level in which there is no sensory component. For example, Alpert and Silvers (1970) compared hallucinations in schizophrenic and alcoholic patients. They conclude that the hallucinations of alcoholics are more sensory, while those of schizophrenics are more cognitive. Thus the voices heard by the alcoholics were more likely to "be localised in space and to emerge from a background of noises and unintelligible voices". In contrast, "the hallucinations of the schizophrenics have a cognitive taint, appearing more like thoughts that have become audible. Thus, schizophrenics report greater intelligibility to their messages, (and) poorer localisation ..."

There is some direct evidence that alcoholic hallucinations have a sensory basis. Gross et al. (1963) and Saravay and Pardes (1967) found that these experiences were associated with a middle ear disorder that leads to rushing noises and clicks. It is these genuine, but internal, noises which "drive" the hallucinations. A similar distinction between sensory and cognitive bases for hallucinations has long been made in the German literature. Exogenous hallucinations—those associated with an obvious organic basis—are considered to have strong sensory components whereas the endogenous hallucinations of schizophrenia do not. Schröder (1926), quoted by Albert (1987), claims that "patients with an endogenous paranoid psychosis can never give descriptions of the wording, tone, direction or strength of the voices". This is an extreme claim, but I believe it probably applies to many of the "auditory hallucinations" described by schizophrenic patients. In Chapter 7 I shall suggest a basis for these experiences which have the content of a verbal communication without any sensory components.

DELUSIONS

Just as hallucinations have been defined as false perceptions, delusions have been defined as false beliefs. There are several possible routes to a false belief, but most theories assume that delusions arise because of impairments in the logical processes of deduction and inference. A critical question for research is whether the fault does actually lie in these processes or elsewhere. In fact there is little evidence that a fault in logical processes causes delusions.

Abnormal Perception + Normal Logic = Delusions

According to one view (Maher, 1974), delusions arise when a patient applies normal logic to an aberrant experience or perception. Thus, someone who is hearing voices may deduce that a group of scientists have invented a special machine that "broadcasts" these voices and believes that these scientists are now experimenting on him/her using this machine. Such a system for explaining an abnormal experience is compellingly described in Evelyn Waugh's semi-autobiographical novel, *The ordeal of Gilbert Pinfold*. While on a cruise shortly after the end of the Second World War, Gilbert Pinfold starts hearing voices:

> For a long time, two hours perhaps, Mr Pinfold lay in his bunk listening. He was able to hear quite distinctly not only what was said in his immediate vicinity, but elsewhere. He had the light on, now, in his cabin and as he gazed at the complex of tubes and wires that ran across his ceiling, he realized that they must form some sort of general junction in the system of communication. Through some trick or fault or wartime survival everything spoken in the executive quarters of the ship was transmitted to him. (Waugh, 1957)

This explanation of delusions works well in cases where the patient clearly has a primary symptom, such as an auditory hallucination, which they are trying to rationalise. It works less well in cases where there is no obvious perceptual abnormality that needs to be explained. On the other hand, it would be very difficult to prove that there were really no perceptual abnormalities in these cases. This theory also predicts that normal people should develop delusions if they are subjected to abnormal experiences. Experiments along these lines would obviously be unethical. The impression from anecdotal evidence is, however, that normal people do not hold any delusional explanations for so long or with such fervour, as do psychotic patients. The theory would also be disproved if it could be shown that patients with delusions have abnormal logic. Such a demonstration would also provide an alternative explanation for the development of delusions.

Abnormal Logic

If perceptions and experiences are normal, then delusions must arise from the abnormal use of this information. In essence, this means that some information is ignored while the rest is over-emphasised. Brennan and Hemsley (1984) have suggested that underlying delusions in patients are the same mechanisms that underlie "illusory correlations" in normal people. People often believe in non-existent relationships between events, through failing to put sufficient weight on counter-examples. In other words, having once formed a hypothesis (in response to coincidental conjunctions) this hypothesis is maintained in spite of counter evidence, "It is the nature of an hypothesis, when once a man has conceived it, that it assimilates everything to itself, as proper nourishment; and, from the first moment of your begetting it, it generally grows the stronger by everything you see, hear, read, or understand. This is of great use" (Lawrence Sterne, 1760). Are paranoid delusions perhaps are a very exaggerated form of this natural human tendency?

David Hemsley and his colleagues have investigated various aspects of logical reasoning in deluded patients. Brennan and Hemsley (1984) found that paranoid patients perceived illusory correlations between pairs of words that had only appeared together at random, particularly when these words related to their delusions. Hemsley and Garety (1986) have suggested that some delusions result from deficits in the ability to weigh new evidence and adjust beliefs accordingly. In consequence, paranoid patients should be impaired in making probability judgments. Huq et al. (1988) and Garety, Hemsley, & Wesseley (1991) have confirmed this prediction and also found that deluded patients were over-confident about conclusions drawn from limited information.

If deluded patients have a general problem with making logical inferences and judgments about probability, then we would expect the content of their delusions to cover a very wide spectrum. In practice, however, the content of delusions is rather narrow. As Bentall et al. (1991b) put it, "... the delusions experienced by psychotic patients seem to concern the patient's place in the social universe". This observation very much goes against the notion that there is a general failure of reasoning in deluded patients. Rather, it suggests that reasoning fails only in relation to the understanding of human interactions. This specificity applies also to experiments on reasoning in deluded patients. Brennan and Hemsley (1984), for example, found that "illusory correlations" were most marked for words with specific paranoid content. Bentall et al. (1991b) found evidence that social reasoning is abnormal in deluded patients and Cutting and Murphy (1990b) found that schizophrenic patients have specific impairments of social knowledge (e.g. How would you tell a friend, politely, that he had stayed too long?) Unfortunately, Cutting and Murphy did not relate this impairment to particular symptoms.

There is a major problem with the notion that delusions reflect the faulty application of logic. Ample research on normal people (e.g. Johnson-Laird, 1982) has shown that the faultless application of logic is not a common feature of human thinking. Most problems are solved on the basis of knowledge drawn from experience rather than reasoning. In circumstances where logic and reasoning have to be used, even those with special training may fare very badly. On this basis we might even argue that what is wrong with many schizophrenic patients is that they are trying to apply logic in circumstances where normal people would not. It seems likely that in most situations where complex inferential processes have to be applied, we use special-purpose cognitive modules, rather than conscious reasoning processes. In Chapter 7 I shall consider the specific cognitive processes that are relevant to social reasoning. I believe that it is impairments in exactly these cognitive processes that lead to delusions.

The theories about delusions that I have considered so far were essentially concerned with paranoid delusions, that is delusions of persecution (Example 5.1 g). However, symptoms classified as delusions are a very mixed bag. Example 5.1 lists some typical delusions associated with schizophrenia. Paranoid delusions (5.1 g) are probably the most familiar. These are false beliefs about other people. So are delusions of reference (5.1 f). Another group of symptoms are sometimes called passivity experiences: alien control (5.1 e), thought insertion (5.1 d) and thought withdrawal. These are labelled delusions because the patient believes that "alien forces are controlling his actions"; this is clearly a false belief. Closer examination, however, suggests that this is not so much a belief, as an experience. For example, in describing thought withdrawal, a patient may say that they can feel the thoughts being sucked out of their mind. Another type of delusion concerns believing that others can hear your thoughts as if they were spoken aloud. This might also be essentially an abnormal experience. Perhaps it is the same experience that leads, in another patient, to the hallucination, "I hear my own thoughts as if they were spoken aloud" (5.1 c). Thus some delusions may reflect weird experiences while others (particularly delusions of persecution and reference) may genuinely reflect faulty inferences: abnormal processes of deduction that lead to false beliefs.

Delusions of Control as Defects in Central Monitoring

I have suggested that some delusions, such as delusions of control by alien forces and thought insertion, are not false beliefs, but reflections of abnormal experiences. Thought insertion, in particular, is an experience that is difficult to understand. Patients say that thoughts that are not their own are coming into their head. This experience implies that we have some way of recognising our own thoughts. It is as if each thought has a label on it saying "mine". If this labelling process goes wrong, then the thought would be perceived as alien.

This idea may sound fanciful when applied to thoughts. However there is ample evidence that such labelling does occur for various simple actions such as eye movements and limb movements. The mechanism by which these responses are labelled has been called "corollary discharge" (Sperry, 1950) or "re-afference copy" (von Holst & Mittelstaedt, 1950). I have already discussed the role of this mechanism in eye movements and speech in the section on auditory hallucinations. A similar mechanism for monitoring all our actions would be of great importance for interpreting our perception of change.

Changes due to outside agencies require different responses to changes brought about by our own actions. An impairment in the ability to distinguish changes due to our own actions and changes due to external events would severely disrupt behaviour and our understanding of the world. I have proposed that it is an impairment in this system that underlies many of the positive symptoms of schizophrenia (Frith, 1987). I believe, however, that it is not only monitoring of action that is impaired in schizophrenia. In addition, it is the monitoring of the intentions to act. I am essentially describing two steps in a central monitoring system. First, the relationship between actions and external events are monitored in order to distinguish between events caused by our own actions and by external agencies. This enables us to know about the causes of events. Second, intentions are monitored in order to distinguish between actions caused by our own goals and plans (willed actions) and actions that are in response to external events (stimulus-driven actions). Such monitoring is essential if we are to have some awareness of the causes of our actions. Given (as we have seen in Chapter 4) that different parts of the brain are concerned with willed action and with stimulus-driven action, this distinction could be made simply on the basis of which brain system was active. Feinberg (1978) has suggested that monitoring mechanisms like corollary discharge apply not only to overt movements of limbs and eyes, but also to covert actions such as thinking. I have illustrated this monitoring system in Figure 5.1 and shown how it relates to the two routes to action shown in Figure 4.1.

How could failures of central monitoring give rise to schizophrenic symptoms? I have suggested previously (Frith, 1987; see also Feinberg, 1978) that a failure to monitor intentions to act would result in delusions of control and other passivity experiences. Thinking, like all our actions, is normally accompanied by a sense of effort and deliberate choice as we move from one thought to the next. If we found ourselves thinking without any awareness of the sense of effort that reflects central monitoring, we might well experience these thoughts as alien and, thus, being inserted into our minds. Similarly actions would appear to be

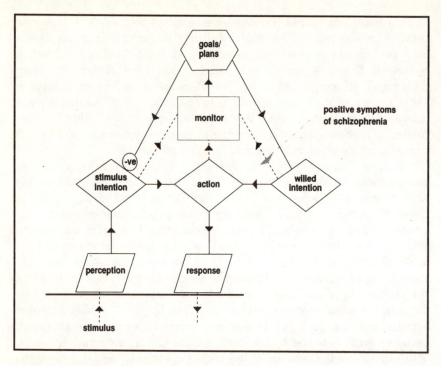

FIG 5.1 The monitoring of action. The monitor receives information about willed intentions, stimulus intentions, and selected actions. One disconnection is shown: information about willed intentions fails to reach the monitor leading to positive symptoms of schizophrenia.

determined by external forces if there was no awareness of the intention to act.

Likewise, if we could not distinguish between events caused by our own actions and those of external origin, then we might attribute events caused by our own actions to external events (or vice versa). One manifestation of this effect would be auditory hallucinations. The patient hears a voice and does not recognise it as their own.

At least two experiments have found evidence that central monitoring is faulty in schizophrenia (Frith & Done, 1989; Malenka et al., 1982). In both these experiments subjects had to follow a target on a computer screen by moving a joystick. The tasks were designed so that subjects frequently made errors by moving the joystick in the wrong direction. Of particular interest was the ability of patients to correct these errors rapidly in the absence of visual feedback. Normal people can correct such errors very rapidly even before they can see the consequence of their error (Megaw, 1972; Rabbitt, 1966). It is argued that the ability of people to make these very rapid error corrections in the absence of external feedback demonstrates that they are monitoring the response intended (via corollary discharge) and thus do not need to wait for external feedback about the response that actually occurred. In other words we can be aware that an intended response was wrong after we have initiated that response, but before the consequences of that response are visible. If certain patients cannot monitor their own intentions, then they should be unable to make these rapid error corrections.

Malenka and his colleagues (1982) found that schizophrenic patients were less likely than normal and alcoholic people to correct their errors in the absence of visual feedback. John Done and I (Frith & Done, 1989) used a very similar task disguised as a video game. We confirmed that acute schizophrenic patients corrected their errors exactly like normal people when visual feedback was supplied but, unlike normal people, often failed to correct errors when there was no feedback. Of particular interest was the observation that this disability was restricted to the patients with passivity experiences: delusions of control, thought insertion and thought blocking. These are precisely the symptoms that can most readily be explained in terms of a defect of self-monitoring.

Janez Mlakar (personal communication) used a different technique for studying central monitoring of actions. Subjects were asked to copy simple geometric designs into a computer by moving a joystick or pressing keys. In one condition the results of their actions appeared on the screen, while in another condition they could not see the figure their movements were producing. In this latter condition correct production of the figure will depend, to a much greater extent, upon central monitoring. Mlakar found that schizophrenic patients with first rank symptoms were much more impaired than other schizophrenic patients when performance depended upon central monitoring.

Rudolph Cohen (1991) has studied slow, response-related negativities in the EEGs of schizophrenic patients. These slow, negative potentials occur after the subject has responded to a stimulus and reflect the subject's degree of uncertainty about the appropriateness of their response. Thus, these potentials reflect some aspect of response monitoring. Cohen suggests that the abnormalities in these potentials observed in acute schizophrenic patients reflect failure of these patients to monitor and appraise their own actions.

All these results confirm that there is an impairment of self-monitoring: this impairment would lead to a lack of awareness of their intended actions and could thus underlie some of the abnormal experiences described by schizophrenic patients.

DOES A SINGLE COGNITIVE DEFICIT UNDERLIE ALL POSITIVE SYMPTOMS?

This self-monitoring theory was originally developed to explain delusions such as thought insertion and alien control. However, it can also explain certain auditory hallucinations, particularly "hearing one's own thoughts spoken aloud" (Example 5.1 c). Indeed, my formulation of a self-monitoring defect has much in common with Richard Bentall's (1990) proposal that auditory hallucinations reflect a defect in reality discrimination. Bentall proposes that hallucinations arise because the patient does not distinguish between external stimuli and internally generated thoughts and memories. Thus a single cognitive defect can explain some hallucinations and some delusions.

However, there are still aspects of both hallucinations and delusions that these formulations do not explain very well. For example, if hallucinations are our own thoughts perceived as coming from an external source, why do these thoughts sometimes take the form of commentaries about us in the third person (Example 5.1 b)? Why should lack of awareness of our own intentions lead to delusions of persecution? Even within the domain of self-monitoring, it seems unlikely that the same system of corollary discharge would relate equally to limb movements as to speech acts. In Chapter 7 I shall suggest that self-monitoring is a special case of a more general cognitive process that has a special role in conscious awareness. I shall propose that all schizophrenic symptoms can be explained in terms of various defects in this process.

THE BRAIN SYSTEMS ASSOCIATED WITH POSITIVE SYMPTOMS

Patients with signs and symptoms meeting all the criteria for schizophrenia are sometimes found to have clear-cut organic illnesses (e.g. Johnstone et al., 1988). However, the nature of these illnesses and the location of the associated brain damage can vary widely. In a study of the whole range of psychoses, Feinstein and Ron (1990) concluded that there was no simple relationship between diagnosis and location of damage. This contrasts with the conclusions of others who believe that some psychotic symptoms can be related to localised brain damage. For example, Trimble (1990) observed that patients with psychosis associated with epilepsy frequently had first rank symptoms (see Example 5.1). His data suggest that these particular symptoms are closely related to temporal lobe pathology, usually in the dominant hemisphere.

There have been many inconclusive studies in which associations have been sought between symptoms or diagnosis and specific locations of brain damage. A frequent, if not perseverative theme in this book is that this search for associations will not be fruitful. Relations are more likely to be found if we consider cognitive processes rather than symptoms. I have suggested that one cognitive process likely to be relevant to positive symptoms is that by which we become aware of our own intentions. I shall therefore consider some neurological patients in whom this process seems to be impaired.

Action Without Awareness

Delusions of control refer to experiences in which the patient feels that their thoughts, acts or emotions are being controlled by external forces rather than by their own will. There is one neurological phenomenon, the alien hand sign, in which the patient actually performs unintended acts. Goldberg et al. (1981) have described two of these cases and propose that they are usually associated with unilateral damage to the medial frontal lobe, most probably the supplementary motor area. The alien hand sign is a disconnection syndrome in which the hand opposite to the lesion shows motor perseveration, forced grasping and apparently purposeful behaviour without conscious volition or knowledge on the part of the patient. Patients find the behaviour of their "alien hand" very disturbing and often hold it down with their other good hand to prevent its movements, rather as Dr Strangelove held his artificial arm in Stanley Kubrick's film.

The alien hand sign has two abnormal components. First, the alien hand performs acts in situations where such acts do not normally occur. Second, the patient is not aware of the intended or actual actions of the hand, unless actually looking at the hand. I believe that the movements of the hand are directly elicited by irrelevant stimuli. For example, if the patient sees a door knob then the hand will grasp it, simply because door knobs are for grasping. This is an example of the "utilisation behaviour" described by Lhermitte (1983), which I discussed in Chapter 4. The question then remains as to why these stimulus-elicited actions are not accompanied by a conscious feeling of intendedness or what Helmholtz (1866) called "effort of will". One possibility might be that this lack of awareness is a general consequence of the brain damage. However, I believe it is more likely that, even in the intact brain, stimulus-elicited actions are not normally accompanied by a feeling of effort or intendedness. Such feelings only occur if the stimulus-driven action has been deliberately permitted, in a situation when it could have been suppressed.

Patients with the alien hand sign have suffered damage to the part of the brain that normally monitors, i.e. permits or suppresses, stimulus-elicited actions in the hand. As a consequence the hand is "released" to perform precisely those actions that we normally perform without awareness.

In terms of this analysis, the alien hand sign is the opposite of the experience associated with delusions of control. Underlying delusions of control, I suggest, is a loss of the feeling of effort or intendedness that is normally associated with willed actions. Underlying the alien hand sign is the release of actions that are not normally accompanied with a feeling of effort or intendedness.

Hershberger and Misceo (1983) have discussed in detail the situations in which movements occur without awareness. They suggest that there are two forms of "efference copy" or "corollary discharge", one of which is automatic and unregistered and the other monitored consciously. My analysis of the alien hand sign is consistent with my conjecture that an impairment in the registering of the sensed form of corollary discharge underlies at least some of the abnormal experiences described by schizophrenic patients. In Figure 5.2 I have illustrated how this sensed form of corollary discharge might fit into to the system for monitoring action illustrated in Figure 5.1.

Blindsight is another example of action without awareness (Weiskrantz, 1980). Patients with lesions in the occipital pole have an area in their visual field in which they are unaware of seeing anything. Nevertheless, they can point to objects in this blind area with some accuracy. David Milner and his colleagues (1991) have described a patient with a different form of blindsight resulting in a more specific lack of awareness of visual form. This defect resulted from damage in the temporo-occipital junction. This patient was unable to match the orientation of a line, but could orientate her hand correctly in order to place it in a slot. This result is consistent with various studies that have shown that different aspects of visual information: colour, movement, and form, for example, are separated in primary visual cortex and channelled to different parts of the extra-striate cortex (Zeki, 1978). There are also pathways from the retina that bypass the occipital cortex altogether. These studies of patients with blindsight show not only that some of these information pathways can be damaged while others remain intact, but also that some of these pathways reach consciousness while others do not. We still do not know what distinguishes the conscious and the unconscious systems.

Weiskrantz (1987) suggests that the amnesic syndrome resembles blindsight because the amnesic patient also acquires knowledge without awareness. Such patients can learn something new, but cannot remember that they have learned it. Weiskrantz considers that

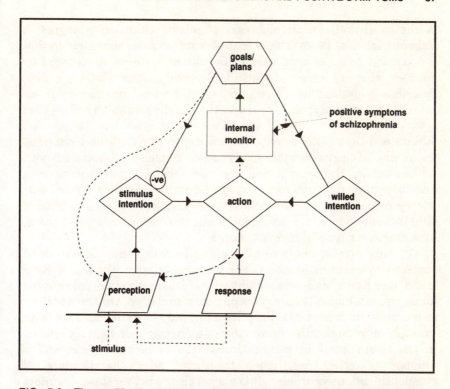

FIG. 5.2   The modification of internal and external monitoring by corollary discharge. The internal monitor receives information about intended action, which is modified by information about goals and plans. The external monitor (perception) is modified by information about goals and plans and current action at an unconscious level. This is achieved by a comparator signal indicating expected actions. One disconnection is shown. If the information about goals and plans fails to modify internal monitoring, then positive psychotic symptoms are experienced.

blindsight and the amnesic syndrome both reflect defects in a similar process of self-monitoring. He considers that this kind of self-awareness is the essence of consciousness. In its most highly developed human form this self-awareness permits us to reflect not only on what we ourselves are thinking, but also on what other people are thinking about us. Weiskrantz suggests that it is defects in this uniquely human ability that can lead to paranoia. I shall discuss this aspect of self-awareness in more detail in Chapter 7.

Perception Without Awareness?

A very specific type of delusion is seen in neurological patients and also schizophrenic patients'—delusional misidentification. Capgras' syndrome is the most well known delusion of misidentification (Capgras & Reboul-Lachaux, 1923). The essential feature of the syndrome is that the patient believes that people they know have been replaced by doubles who are almost identical physically. John Cutting (1990) describes a patient who sustained right parietal damage after an overdose of amitriptyline. "For several weeks she refused to believe that I was the real Dr Cutting who had looked after her before. She maintained that I was physically identical to him, but more outgoing than him." Capgras' syndrome is most frequently associated with schizophrenia. However, it has also been observed in patients with known organic damage, as in the case described by Cutting. In their survey of patients with Alzheimer's disease, Burns, Jacoby, & Levy (1990) found evidence of misidentification of people in 12% of cases, including one case of Capgras' syndrome.

Not only people, but also places and buildings can appear to be replaced by identical doubles. For example, Kapur, Turner, & King (1988) describe a man with a right frontal lesion who insisted that his house was not his real house. This patient also claimed that he had been in ten different hospitals although he had only been in one. This is an example of "reduplicative paramnesia", a phenomenon long recognised in the neurological literature. Joseph (1986) brought these and a number of other syndromes together under the heading of misidentification syndromes. It is not yet clear whether these disorders can be related to damage in particular brain systems. Right hemisphere damage seems to be a common feature. Alexander, Stuss, & Benson (1979) consider that a combination of bilateral frontal and right hemisphere damage is present for all types of misidentification syndrome.

Ellis and Young (1990) have discussed delusional misidentifications in terms of the cognitive processes that underlie face and object recognition. Their explanation of misidentifications has interesting parallels to my account, in the previous section, of disorders in the experience of action. Ellis and Young's account of Capgras' syndrome is based on the proposition that there are several independent modules concerned with different aspects of face processing. These include face recognition units, person identity nodes, and expression analysis. Because these modules are independent, they provide different routes by which a face can be recognised. Ellis and Young consider two routes in particular. One route permits a face to be identified while the other permits a face to be recognised as familiar and may also attach some emotional tone. In part, the evidence for these two routes comes from studies of prosopagnosic patients. These patients are unable to identify faces, even those of their immediate family. However, they can distinguish between familiar and unfamiliar faces (Bauer, 1984). Thus, in these cases, only one of the two routes to face recognition has been damaged.

Bauer (1984) has suggested that two different anatomical pathways underlie these two routes. Face identification depends on a ventral pathway from visual cortex to temporal lobes. The feeling of familiarity depends on a dorsal pathway leading from the visual cortex to the limbic system via the inferior parietal lobule. Ellis and Young suggest that Capgras' syndrome is the mirror image of prosopagnosia. The route to identification remains intact, but the route concerned with feelings of familiarity and emotional tone is damaged. As a consequence the patient can identify the face of his wife, but no longer recognises her as being familiar or arousing any emotion. The person he sees looks like his wife, but he does not "know" her. He infers that this is not his wife, but some duplicate. Damage to a slightly different area might lead to the same discrepant perception when the patient enters his house. It looks like his house, but it is not familiar. Once again he concludes that it must be a copy.

It seems to me that this formulation has marked parallels with my account of delusions of control, in which actions occur without any feeling of intendedness. In this case the patient acts, but this is not accompanied with an awareness of "intention". In the case of misidentification the patient perceives, but this perception is not accompanied by a feeling of "knowing". I shall consider these defects of self-awareness further in Chapter 7. In both cases medial brain systems seem to be involved, probably including the limbic system.

Role of Dopamine in the Control of Positive Symptoms

Another clue we have about the brain systems underlying positive symptoms comes from the therapeutic effectiveness of dopamine-blocking drugs, which I discussed in Chapter 2. Treatment with these drugs can markedly reduce the severity of positive symptoms (hallucinations, delusions, and thought disorder), but has little or no effect on negative signs (e.g. Johnstone et al., 1978b). In Chapter 4, I discussed the role of dopamine in the generation of willed action. I suggested that reduction of dopaminergic activity, as happens in Parkinson's disease, or after treatment with antipsychotics, should reduce the ability of the subject to generate willed actions. In other words, dopamine-blocking drugs should, if anything, exacerbate negative signs. Why then should they have any effect on positive symptoms?

I have suggested that certain positive symptoms occur because patients act without being aware of any intention to act. The patients have abnormal experiences because of the discrepancy between what they are doing and their awareness of what they intended to do. In Figure 5.2 I have illustrated the two relevant pathways that feed information into the central monitor. Discrepancies occur because of impairments in one of these pathways. There are two ways in which this discrepancy can be rectified. First the damaged pathway can be repaired. At present we do not know where this pathway is, let alone how to repair it. However, the discrepancy can also be reduced by cutting down activity in the intact pathway. Abnormal experiences occur whenever a patient performs an act without being aware of their intention. If the patient did not perform the act in the first place, then the problem would not arise.

Thus, one way in which dopamine-blocking drugs might ameliorate positive symptoms is by reducing the patient's spontaneous activity. If there is no willed action, then there is no opportunity to experience acts as controlled by alien forces. If this account is correct, then there will, of necessity, be a price to pay for the success of antipsychotic medication that is based on dopamine blockade. Positive symptoms will be reduced, but the patient will find it more difficult to think and act spontaneously. This is a problem well known to clinicians. Difficulties with thinking and concentration are frequently reported by patients treated with antipsychotic drugs (Hirsch, 1982). In many cases patients will cease taking the drugs because of these unfortunate side-effects.

Animal Models for Positive Symptoms

Positive symptoms are much more difficult to study than negative signs. Negative signs can be observed; we cannot observe positive symptoms, we depend on the patient telling us about them. Thus, while we can have an animal model of negative signs like poverty of action, stereotyped behaviour or social withdrawal, we cannot have an animal model of a positive symptom. However, it is possible to study in animals some of the cognitive processes that might underlie positive symptoms.

In this chapter I have suggested that certain delusions and hallucinations occur because of an impairment in the patient's ability to monitor their own actions. Experiments on this kind of self-monitoring have been successfully performed with animals. For example, Beninger and his colleagues (1974) taught rats to obtain food rewards by monitoring their own activity. The rats had four different levers to press. Each lever corresponded to one of four different acts that rats frequently carry out quite naturally: face washing, rearing up, walking, and remaining immobile. The rat could perform any of these acts whenever it wished. However, only if it pressed the correct lever after performing an act would it get a food reward. As the rats could learn how to get the food rewards, they must have been able to monitor their own activity and remember what it was they had just done.

I have suggested that self-monitoring is important because it permits animals to distinguish between events that have been caused by their own actions and events that have external causes. Robinson and Wurtz (1976) have identified cells in the superficial layer of the superior colliculus of the rhesus monkey that distinguish between real and self-induced stimulus movement. These cells respond to rapid stimulus movements, but do not respond when the monkey moves its eye past a stationary stimulus. This is in marked contrast to cells in the striate cortex, which do not distinguish between stimulus movement and eye movement conditions. On the other hand, cells in the striate cortex are very sensitive to different visual features while the collicular cells are very poorly tuned to stimulus features. Robinson and Wurtz conclude that the input to the superior colliculus that permits the detection of real stimulus movement is a corollary discharge from some part of the oculomotor system. They tentatively identify the frontal eye field as the most likely source of this information. It is possible that it is these frontal systems that generate the conscious "sense of effort" that I believe to be abnormal in schizophrenia.

Ploog (1979) has described a similar system that permits the monkey to distinguish between self-generated and externally produced vocalisations. Müller-Preuss (1978) has identified cells in the auditory cortex of the squirrel monkey which respond to loudspeaker-transmitted vocalisations, but not to self-produced vocalisations. Ploog concludes that the inhibition of these cells during self-produced calling is caused by corollary discharges associated with vocalisation. He tentatively suggests that the anterior cingulate cortex is a possible source of this information (Müller-Preuss et al., 1980). Müller-Preuss and Jürgens (1976) have described in some detail a "cingulate vocalisation system". They sugge. ; that the anterior cingulate cortex is the source of willed vocalisations and demonstrate the existence of connections from this structure not only to Broca's area (Brodmann's area 44), traditionally associated with speech production, but also auditory association areas, including Wernicke's area (Brodmann's area 22), associated with speech perception.

Although there is, as yet, relatively little work on the self-monitoring of perception and action in animals, it is clear from the examples I have quoted, that the methodology for conducting the necessary experiments is already available. In Chapter 4, I suggested that certain anterior brain structures: dorsolateral prefrontal cortex, supplementary motor area, and anterior cingulate cortex, were involved in the generation of willed action. It is, perhaps, not surprising that similar areas: frontal eye field and anterior cingulate cortex, are thought to be the sources of the corollary discharges that tell us whether our perceptions are self-generated or from some external source. In Figure 5.3 I provide a very speculative attempt to map the cognitive processes underlying self-monitoring of speech onto brain structures. This is largely based on the work by Jürgens and his colleagues on the squirrel monkey (Jürgens, 1986). It is possible that the homologue of the monkey "anterior cingulate vocalisation area" in man is the anterior part of the

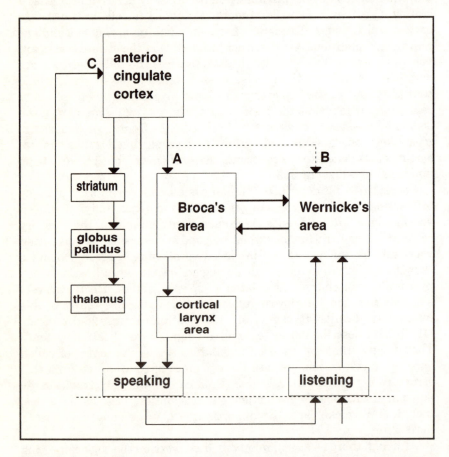

FIG. 5.3 Control of vocalisation. The anterior cingulate cortex controls vocalisation (A). It modifies speech perception by corollary discharge (B) and is itself modified by the striatal loop (C).

supplementary motor area. Given this possibility, it is interesting that SMA is active when human volunteers merely think of words, rather than saying them out loud (Wise et al., 1991). As we have seen, it is this "inner speech" that is likely to be associated with auditory hallucinations.

These speculations suggest a relationship between the positive and the negative features of schizophrenia in terms of severity of the underlying brain abnormality. Positive symptoms occur because the brain structures responsible for willed actions no longer send corollary discharges to the posterior parts of the brain concerned with perception. This would be caused by disconnections between these brain regions. In consequence self-generated changes in perception are misinterpreted as having an external cause. If the structures responsible for action are more severely damaged then messages are no longer sent to the brain structures concerned with response generation either. This results in a lack of willed action and hence the negative features of schizophrenia.

CHAPTER 6

Communication in Schizophrenia

Language and speech in schizophrenia have been studied more than any other feature. The things that schizophrenic patients say can have all the bizarreness of the positive symptoms, hallucinations and delusions, but, unlike these symptoms, can be studied directly. Some schizophrenic patients say things that are barely comprehensible, but very fascinating. It is easy to believe that, if we could understand what they are saying, we would also understand "schizophrenia" (see Example 6.1)

Example 6.1 (from Bleuler, 1913)

Then, I always liked geography. My last teacher in the subject was Professor August A. He was a man with black eyes. I also like black eyes. There are also blue and gray eyes and other sorts, too. I have heard it said that snakes have green eyes. All people have eyes. There are some, too, who are blind. These blind people are led by a boy. It must be terrible not to be able to see. There are people who can't see, and, in addition, can't hear. I know some who hear too much. There are many sick people in Burgholzli; they are called patients.

Schizophrenic speech can also be deviant without being incomprehensible. Table 6.1 lists the deviant aspects of language most frequently observed in Nancy Andreasen's classic study of language and communication in psychotic patients (Andreasen, 1979).

Table 6.1
Types of deviant language observed in patients with schizophrenia.
Examples are from Andreasen (1979) unless otherwise stated

Poverty of speech (29%)	Monosyllabic answers (see Example 4.1)
Poverty of content of speech (40%)	Replies of adequate length supplying little information. 'Tell me what kind of a person you are.' 'Ah one hell of an odd thing to say perhaps in these particular circumstances. I happen to be quite pleased with who I am or how I am and many of the problems that I have and have been working on are difficult for me to handle or to work on because I am not aware of them as problems which upset me personally.
Tangentiality (36%)	Oblique or irrelevant replies. 'What city are you from?' '... I was born in Iowa, but I know that I'm white instead of black so apparently I came from the north somewhere and I don't know where, you know, I really don't know where my ancestors came from ...'
Derailment (56%)	Lack of proper connection between phrases and ideas. 'How are things at home?' 'What I'm saying is my mother is too ill. No money. It all comes out of her pocket. My flat's leaking. It's ruined my mattress. It's Lambeth council. I'd like to know what the caption in the motto under their coat of arms is. It's in Latin ...' (Cutting, 1985)
Incoherence (16%)	Unintelligible, lack of proper connection between words (see Example 1.1)
Illogicality (27%)	'Parents can be anything, material, vegetable or mineral, that has taught you something'
Loss of goal (44%)	Failure to follow a chain of thought through to its natural conclusion (see Example 6.1)
Perseveration (24%)	Persistent repetition of words or ideas (see Example 6.2)
Self-reference (13%)	Repeatedly referring the subject under discussion back to the self. 'What time is it?' 'Seven o'clock. That's my problem. I never know what time it is. Maybe I should try to keep better track of the time.'

Like the other signs and symptoms of schizophrenia, these abnormalities of language fall naturally into positive and negative groups. Poverty of speech and poverty of content of speech are obviously "negative", while most of the other features such as incoherence and derailment are abnormal by their presence and thus positive.

Thought Disorder or Language Disorder?

The peculiar speech observed in many schizophrenic patients is traditionally labelled "thought disorder". This label suggests that the peculiar things that schizophrenic patients say are a consequence of peculiar thoughts. The label further suggests that the ability to put these thoughts into language is unimpaired. So far this assumption remains unproven. Indeed, first-person accounts suggest that some patients at least do experience difficulty in putting their thoughts into language.

Frequently, patients express abnormal thoughts in normal language. Hence the expression of the false beliefs associated with delusions can be understood as a consequence of abnormal thought processes. For instance, one patient told me, "the reason I get sunburn is because people are lying under sun-ray lamps and thinking about me." Psychiatrists therefore distinguish between disturbances of the content and the form of thought.

If a patient has "formal thought disorder", then it is not necessarily the content of their thoughts that is abnormal. It may be the form in which the thoughts are expressed that is abnormal. In this case there are abnormalities in the language used to express the thoughts. There is a fundamental difference between language and thought, which has received surprisingly little emphasis in the study of schizophrenia. Thinking is a private matter, whereas language is arguably the most important method we have for communicating with others. Thus language is not simply the expression of thoughts; it is the expression of thoughts in a manner designed to communicate these thoughts to others

Language or Communication?

There have been a number of studies of language disorders in schizophrenia that have looked for defects at different linguistic levels. Psycholinguists have proposed that the production of language depends on the interaction of a series of relatively independent modules. For example, Butterworth (1985, Figure 3.1) describes six such systems; phonetic, phonological, prosodic, syntactic, lexical, and semantic. Although all these processes can be impaired independently, they can all be modulated from the highest level. For example, to indicate that we are reporting somebody else's words, we might alter our phonology. We adopt a higher pitch, for example. This is an example of how a low level system can be used to carry information about a higher order aspect of communication.

Many studies have been carried out on different levels of language function in schizophrenic patients. In most of these studies specific defects in lower level processes have not been found. For example, Andreasen and her colleagues (1985) investigated three different aspects of language: syntax (grammar), semantics (meaning), and discourse (how phrases and sentences are linked together). They concluded that schizophrenic patients showed specific impairments only at the level of discourse. In their words the schizophrenic patients were defective in their use of "rules governing the manner in which sentences may be combined to construct an idea set or story". Frith and Allen (1988) reviewed studies of language in schizophrenia and concluded that "lexical and syntactic knowledge structures were intact", but that "there was a failure to structure discourse at higher levels". McGrath (1991) concluded that the key feature of formal thought disorder was "a lack of executive planning and editing".

Thus the general consensus is that only the highest levels of language processes are impaired in schizophrenia. This does not mean that there will be no errors at the lower levels listed by Butterworth (lexical, syntactic, semantic, etc.). Rather it means that, in schizophrenia, errors at these levels can be explained as the consequence of higher level processing failure.

What are these high level processes of "discourse" and "planning" that are impaired in schizophrenic language? There are two important points to note. First, a defect in planning must apply to expressive rather than receptive aspects of language. Second, when we talk of incoherent discourse and lack of planning we are describing the problem the listener has in understanding schizophrenic speech. As one of McGhie and Chapman's (1961) patients said, "people listening to me get more lost than I do". The abnormalities of schizophrenic language lie at the level not of language competence, but of language use. The problems arise when the patient has to use language to communicate with others. These problems apply not just to speech, but to all the non-verbal modes of communication as well.

There is direct experimental evidence that schizophrenic language abnormalities are expressive rather than receptive. Cohen (1976) asked volunteers to describe a coloured disk in such a way that a listener would be able to pick out that disk from among other disks of different colours. The results of this experiment were very clear. Communication failed only when it was a schizophrenic patient who was describing the colour. The same patient would have no difficulty in using the description given by a normal control subject.

John Done and I (Done & Frith, 1984) studied the effects of context on the threshold for the detection of single words. If we hear speech in a noisy environment, it is easier to hear the last word in the sentence "coming in he took off his coat" than it is in the sentence "coming in he took off his dance". We found that the effects of context on threshold were the same for the schizophrenic patients as for the normal controls. Differences only emerged when the words were presented below threshold and the subjects had to guess what they were. The guesses made by the patients were abnormal. They were more likely to repeat previous words and also to produce words that were less appropriate to the context. Here again it was only the expressive aspects of single word processing that were abnormal.

The processes by which we use language to communicate our ideas and wishes to others are covered by the term "pragmatics". Grice (1975) has pointed out that communication is essentially a cooperative venture. On this basis he proposed several maxims for successful communication, including: be informative, speak the truth, be relevant, be brief, be orderly. The point of these maxims is that listeners normally assume that a speaker is following them and interpret what they hear accordingly. In schizophrenic speech some or all of these maxims are frequently broken. The major requirement for successful communication is to take account of the knowledge, beliefs, and intentions of the person to whom we are speaking. This is necessary even for quite simple aspects of discourse. A number of studies have shown that "thought-disordered" speakers give inadequate referents and cohesive ties. These features of discourse are essential for the understanding of the listener. Rochester and Martin (1979, p. 106) put it very succinctly, "Speakers tell listeners new things on the basis of what they assume are old things for the listener".

Rochester and Martin give the following example: "There was a donkey about to cross a river. It was loaded with bags of salt." Once the donkey has been introduced into the discourse, then subsequently the donkey can be referred to by the pronoun "it". Schizophrenic patients frequently fail to use pronominal reference correctly (see Frith & Allen, 1988, p. 181); sometimes a pronoun is used without any antecedent. For example, one of Rochester and Martin's patients said, "Ever studied that sort of formation, block of ice in the ground? Well, it fights the permafrost, it pushes it away and lets things go up around it. You can see they're like, they're almost like a pattern with a flower. They start from the middle". This speaker provides no antecedent for "they". Apparently, he assumes that the listener already knows who or what they are. Possibly he had snowflakes in mind.

The opposite pattern can also be observed when the speaker fails to use pronouns. Another of Rochester and Martin's patients said, "I see a woman in the middle of a snow bank—I see a woman in a telephone booth in the middle of a snow bank going yackety yack yack yack." After its first appearance in this passage, the woman could have been replaced by "her". In this example the speaker unnecessarily reminds the listener that he is talking about a woman. His speech is stilted, pedantic, and repetitive.

Among writers on pragmatics, Sperber and Wilson (1986), in particular, have discussed in detail the necessity for speakers and listeners to make inferences about each other's knowledge, beliefs, and intentions. They point out that, for communication to begin, the listener must first recognise the speaker's intention to communicate. The speaker will indicate their intention to communicate in many ways, including non-verbal signals such as coughing or leaning forward. These signals of intent to communicate can be called ostensive signals. I propose that abnormalities in the recognition of ostensive signals can explain two typical features of schizophrenia. If the patient fails to respond to ostensive signals then we observe social withdrawal. In contrast, some patients see ostensive signals where none are intended. Such patients falsely believe that many people are trying to communicate with them. This is an example of delusion of reference.

My conclusion is that some schizophrenic "thought disorder" reflects a disorder of communication, caused in part by a failure of the patient to take account of the listener's knowledge in formulating their speech. This theory explains the asymmetry observed by Cohen, that schizophrenics could understand normals, but normals could not understand schizophrenics. The normal speaker takes account of the listener's lack of knowledge, and thus the schizophrenic listener can understand. The schizophrenic speaker does *not* take account of the listener's lack of knowledge, and thus the listener has difficulty in understanding.

Schizophrenic Speech: One Defect or Many?

There are many different ways of being incomprehensible. Most of these different ways are captured by the signs listed in Table 6.1. With incoherent speech we understand the words, but not how they fit together. With derailment we understand each of the phrases and ideas, but again not how they fit together. With loss of goal the phrases and ideas fit together, but do not lead to any conclusion. There is also the possibility of incomprehension at a pragmatic level. We can understand exactly what the patients are saying, but we have no idea why they are saying it. These different types of incomprehensibility reflect the different type of cognitive abnormality that I have put forward in Chapters 4 and 5. These are disorders of willed action and disorders of monitoring.

DISORDERS OF ACTION

The disorders of action associated with schizophrenia (see Chapter 4) fall into three categories. First, there is poverty of action; no action is produced. Second, there is perseveration; the same action is repeated inappropriately. Third, actions occur which are inappropriate to the context. All three of these abnormalities can be observed in the speech of schizophrenic patients and also in non-verbal aspects of their communication.

Reduced Action

Poverty of speech directly describes the lack of speech production. Even at the level of single word production, abnormalities can be observed in schizophrenic patients. As might be expected, patients with negative signs, particularly poverty of speech, produce fewer words in a given time on tasks such as verbal fluency, e.g. name as many animals as you can in three minutes (Allen & Frith, 1983; Kolb & Wishaw, 1983). As we have already seen in Chapter 4, the reduction in fluency is not simply the consequence of having fewer words available in the lexicon. The schizophrenic patient knows as many words as anyone else, but has difficulty in spontaneously producing words in a given category (Allen, Liddle, & Frith, submitted).

Change can also be observed at the syntactic level. Morice and others have found reduced syntactic complexity in the speech of schizophrenic patients: fewer relative clauses, less clausal embedding, shorter utterances, and so on (Fraser et al., 1986; Morice & Ingram, 1982). The relationship between these speech changes and specific clinical features, such as poverty of speech, were not examined in this study, but this type of speech was found to be associated with long illness and with an early onset of illness. Subsequently, Thomas et al. (1987) found that acute patients with predominantly negative symptoms had speech of lower syntactic complexity than those without. This kind of speech seems to me to be an example of poverty at the level of syntax.

Poverty of content of speech implies many words, but few ideas. Heidi Allen (1983) measured the number of ideas in speech transcripts and found that poverty of ideas was a general feature of the speech of patients who had been ill for a long time, whether they were rated as showing poverty or incoherence of speech. Poverty of action can also be observed in non-verbal components of communication. For example, I consider that the sign "flattening of affect" does not actually refer to affect, but to a lack of expressive use of the face and tone of voice in communication. Leff and Abberton (1981) showed that patients considered to show flattened affect had monotonous voices measurable as a reduction of variation in the pitch of the voice. Murphy and Cutting (1990) showed that acute schizophrenic patients were specifically impaired in the use of prosody (variations in the pitch, intensity, and rhythm of speech) for the expression of emotion. Braun et al. (1991) showed that chronic schizophrenic patients were specifically impaired in using their faces to express emotion.

Perseveration of Action

Poverty of content can also arise because the patient uses rather few words, but repeats them. This can be measured directly using the type/token ratio (the number of different words divided by the total number of words). This ratio is frequently found to be low in schizophrenic speech (Manschrek et al., 1984). These repetitions can be quite subtle or they can be very striking, as in Example 6.2, collected by Heidi Allen, in which a patient is describing a farming scene.

Inappropriate Action

Formal testing of patients rated incoherent, shows that they are producing words that are unusual or inappropriate in the context. In verbal fluency tasks, patients with incoherence produce unusual and

---

Example 6.2 (transcript of a description of a farming scene by a chronic schizophrenic patient. The dashes indicate pauses)

Some—farm houses—in a farm yard—time—with a horse and horseman—time where—going across the field as if they're ploughing the field—time—with ladies—or collecting crops—time work is—coming with another lady—time work is—and where—she's holding a book—time—thinking of things—time work is—and time work is where—you see her coming time work is on the field—and where work is—where her time is where working is and thinking of people and where work is and where you see the hills—going up—and time work is—where you see the—grass—time work is—time work is and where the fields are—where growing is and where work is.

deviant words. This means that they produce words that are very unusual for the category (e.g. "aardvark" for "animals") or words that are not in the category proscribed (e.g. "ginger" as a "fruit'; Allen et al., submitted). In word association tasks with ambiguous words, patients produced associations to the less likely meaning. For example, to the word pair tree–bark, an incoherent patient might give the response "dog" (Allen, 1988). In this case the response given by the patient seems to have been less affected by the context than normal. A popular method of investigating the effect of context on word generation is the "cloze" procedure. In this task, the subject has to fill in the missing words in a passage of text. De Silva and Hemsley (1977) found that acute schizophrenic patients had great difficulty in choosing the correct words in this task. In one version of the task, the missing word is the last word of a phrase or sentence (e.g. He played the gramophone far too ...). John Done and I have also found that incoherent patients completed such sentences with unlikely words.

Spontaneous speech produced by incoherent patients is also characterised by the use of unlikely words. This can be demonstrated by transcribing their speech, striking out some of the words, and asking normal people to fill them in. This task is found to be more difficult than for speech produced by normal people (Manschreck et al., 1979). Thus, whether the context is provided by themselves or by an experimenter, patients with incoherence of speech tend to use unlikely, though usually plausible words.

In some cases, schizophrenic patients generate new words or "neologisms". This can be seen as an extreme case of the use of unlikely words. It is possible that the patient is generating these new words as the best way of expressing some nuance of meaning that is not captured by any existing words. Such new words might be needed to explain the patient's bizarre experiences. However, this subtlety is achieved at the expense of losing the comprehension of the listener. LeVine and Conrad (1979) give a list of 75 neologisms and their definitions generated by a patient whose "voices" were revealing to him a new language (Example 6.3). There was no evidence in this example that the patient was trying to express subtle meanings. Of course, neologisms are sometimes used in literature (e.g. Lewis Carrol in *Jabberwocky*, James Joyce in *Finnegans wake*, and Russel Hoban in *Riddley Walker*), but in these cases the author is careful to explain the new words, or at least to provide a context from which their meaning can be inferred.

Syntax also can be inappropriate rather than restricted. Morice (1986) reports that "a few subjects produced sentences of extraordinary length and complexity (of syntax), well beyond the mean values of the control group". However, these sentences contained many errors.

Example 6.3 Examples of neologisms generated by a chronic schizophrenic
patient (LeVine & Conrad, 1979)

abbliscotage	soup	flopate	fish
blistytake	medicine	gobonbelix	safety
carcitynate	parking place	lancit	string of beans
casilignated	stiff	mulleygully	to be tickled
farato	father	potamtaetash	fertilizer
flattercheflute	talk too much	yanyanta	uncle

Non-verbal aspects of communication have been relatively little studied, but "incongruity of affect" is a well known feature that I believe belongs in the domain of non-verbal communication and refers to production of inappropriate non-verbal signals, rather than inappropriate feelings.

ABNORMALITIES OF SELF-MONITORING

In Chapter 5, I proposed that delusions of alien control and certain auditory hallucinations could be the result of failures in the patient's ability to monitor their own actions. Similar explanations have also been applied to speech abnormalities. I have already referred to the ingenious paradigm developed by Bertram Cohen and his colleagues, in which patients are asked to describe one of a set of coloured patches so that a listener can pick out the patch being described from other, similar patches (Cohen, 1976). In these studies the patients were in the early stages of their first episode of schizophrenia and all showed evidence of language and thought disorder. Rosenberg and Cohen (1966) suggest that, in order to perform this task, the speaker generates a series of descriptions of the target patch. After each possible description is generated there is a self-editing stage "in which the speaker implicitly takes the role of listener in order to 'test' the adequacy of the sampled response before emitting (or rejecting) it". Cohen concludes that schizophrenic patients fail to edit out non-discriminating descriptions. I interpret this phenomenon as a failure of self-monitoring. Example 6.2 shows a patient giving a reasonable description of a picture, but failing to edit out irrelevant, perseverative phrases. Cohen observed that his patients did not simply and rapidly emit a non-discriminating description and then stop. Rather, they emitted a sequence of inadequate descriptions (Example 6.4).

Example 6.4 Attempts to describe one of four coloured disks (Cohen, 1978)

Normal speaker: The lightest of the greens. The others become blue like the ocean or the sea.

Schizophrenic speaker: Clean green. The one without the cream. Don't see this colour on planes, it looks like moss, boss.

Cohen proposed a perseverative-chaining mechanism by which patients emit a series of inadequate responses, each associated with the last response, rather than with the colour patch they are trying to describe. Cohen implies that his patients recognised that their responses were inadequate and thus went on elaborating their replies in the hope of improving the situation. "... There is a futile, but still persisting struggle to communicate adequately."

In Chapter 5, I suggested that patients with certain positive symptoms had difficulty monitoring their own intentions. This proposal could explain Cohen's observations if his patients could only monitor their responses (by peripheral feedback) after they had emitted them. Thus they would recognise that their responses were inadequate, but would not be able to "edit out" these bad responses before they had said them.

As I have already mentioned in Chapter 5, Hoffman (1986) has put forward a theory involving self-monitoring, which explicitly relates speech disorder to auditory hallucinations. Hoffman proposes that the fundamental disorder lies in planning. Schizophrenic discourse is disorganised because many of the utterances of which it is composed do not fit in with the overall goals and plan. Likewise, schizophrenic thinking is disorganised by the occurrence of thoughts that do not fit into the overall plan. Hoffman proposes that, if there is a large discrepancy between the utterance (or thought) and the current cognitive goal, then it is experienced as unintended or "alien". In particular, he suggests that when verbal imagery is experienced as unintended, it is reported as an auditory hallucination. This theory has much in common with my own explanation of certain positive symptoms. In both accounts, there is a failure of self-monitoring so that some self-generated acts are perceived as alien. In Hoffman's account, schizophrenic discourse is disorganised because of frequent intrusions by these "alien" utterances.

Ivan Leudar has examined the role of self-monitoring in schizophrenic speech by studying self-repair. This is a common

---

Example 6.5 Adequate self-repair

The patient is describing the actions of the experimenter so that they could be carried out by a listener. The experimenter puts the red circle on the blue square.
Patient: "Put the red square—red circle—on the blue square."

---

occurrence in normal speech—the speaker recognises an error and corrects it. Leudar and his colleagues (submitted) used a task (Example 6.5) in which subjects had to describe the actions of the experimenter in such a way that a listener could reproduce them. Although the patients produced more faulty and inadequate descriptions than the controls, the proportion of the descriptions that they attempted to repair was the same as the controls. The patients clearly recognised that there was something wrong with their descriptions. However, for many patients, particularly those with hallucinations, the repairs were also wrong or inadequate. Consequently, the repair did not actually improve the communication.

I suspect that Leudar's results are similar to those of Cohen. Both studies suggest that schizophrenic patients recognise that their utterances are faulty. They therefore elaborate them, but these elaborations do not improve matters. The hypothesis of a deficit in internal (or central) monitoring, but not external monitoring can explain these results. According to this hypothesis, patients are only able to check the accuracy of an utterance *after* they have made it. They are not able to edit out faulty utterances *before* they have said them. It is therefore difficult for them to avoid producing a string of faulty utterances, even during attempts at repair (Example 6.6).

ABNORMALITIES IN THE AWARENESS OF OTHERS

The final cause of faulty communication in schizophrenia is that the patient fails to take account of the knowledge of the listener when constructing their utterances. I have already discussed the work of

---

Example 6.6 (from Cohen, 1976)

Too many bloody words all coming to mind. Why don't they stop when all you gotta do is say the lightest green. That's not enough.

Rochester and others, which has demonstrated a lack of referents and of cohesive ties in the utterances of schizophrenic patients. The main function of these devices is to provide a structure for the listener and to indicate when the speaker is introducing knowledge new to the listener and when referring to something the speaker already knows. As yet there is no research that has investigated directly the ability of schizophrenic patients to infer what knowledge is available to their listeners. However, a number of authors have suggested that schizophrenic patients either do not have or do not use this information.

Rutter (1985) analysed a series of conversations between acute schizophrenic patients and nurses. He found abnormalities in the predictability of these discourses, particularly in question and answer sequences. He concluded that "the central problem lies ... in the social process of taking the role of the other".

Harrow and Miller (1985) have concluded that schizophrenic speech appears disjointed to others because the patients do not share "conventional social norms". In other words their discourse is guided, at least in part, by knowledge that is not shared with the listener.

David Good (1990) has discussed repair in conversation in terms of cooperation between speaker and listener and the need of the speaker to supply the knowledge needed by the listener to understand the speaker's utterances. He presents an example in which a schizophrenic speaker provides an inadequate account of a story he has just heard. This speaker behaves as a cooperative conversational partner because he recognises that his listener does not understand. In consequence, he repeatedly attempts to repair the situation. Unfortunately none of these attempts succeed. The patient understands that his listener needs more information, but is apparently unable to discover precisely what information he needs to supply.

Sperber and Wilson (1986) have distinguished between two ways of communicating; decoding and inference. An utterance can be decoded on the basis of its syntax and the meanings of the words of which it is composed. This would give the literal meaning of the utterance, but would not necessarily indicate what the speaker meant. To discover the speaker's meaning we need to take account of the context and make inferences about the speaker's knowledge and intentions. In many cases the literal meaning and the speaker's meaning do not coincide. This is the case in certain figures of speech such as metaphor and irony (Example 6.7).

Schizophrenic patients should have particular difficulty in understanding utterances in which there is a discrepancy between the literal and the intended meaning. Cutting and Murphy (1990a) found that schizophrenic patients do indeed have difficulty with the

Example 6.7. *Utterances in which literal meaning and speaker's meaning do not coincide*

Form	Utterance	Meaning
Interrogative	Can you tidy up this room?	Tidy up this room!
Metaphor	This room is a pigsty	I think this room is very untidy
Irony	This room is so tidy	I am disgusted by the untidiness of this room

metaphorical meanings of words and sentences relative to other psychotic patients. So far, no one has investigated whether or not schizophrenic patients understand irony.

I have suggested reasons for expecting a number of different problems in the language of schizophrenic patients. These are illustrated diagramatically in Figure 6.1. Many students of schizophrenia have emphasised those problems of schizophrenic language that lie in the domain of pragmatics. This implies that schizophrenic patients have problems with making inferences about the knowledge and intentions of their listeners and in using these inferences to guide their discourse plans. In view of the popularity of this hypothesis it is surprising that, as yet, few studies have directly investigated the ability of schizophrenic patients to make inferences about the knowledge of others. In the last few years a wealth of experimental methodology has been developed for studying these processes in children. The same techniques should now be applied to the study of schizophrenia.

BRAIN AND LANGUAGE

Schizophrenic Speech and Aphasia

More is known about the role of the brain in language than in any other aspect of neuropsychology. This knowledge is reflected by the many different kinds of aphasia that have been described. As schizophrenic speech problems are all at the level of output, we would expect them to resemble expressive aphasia. These disorders are associated with left-sided, anterior lesions, particularly in Broca's area. However, the form most frequently seen, nominal aphasia, has little in common with schizophrenic speech. Patients with nominal aphasia have difficulty in finding words and, particularly, with naming objects even though they know what the objects are. Often the problem seems to lie in the stage at which the appropriate phonology for the word has to be generated.

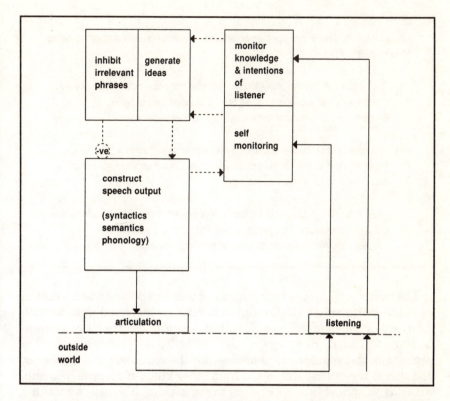

FIG. 6.1 A diagram of the processes involved in producing and monitoring speech. The dotted lines indicate connections, each of which can be impaired in schizophrenia.

The schizophrenic patient does not have these kinds of difficulty. There is, however, one kind of expressive aphasia, jargon aphasia, which, at least on the surface, bears some resemblance to schizophrenic incoherence (Example 6.8). Patients with jargon aphasia also produce incomprehensible speech that includes neologisms (Example 6.9(3)).

Example 6.8 Speech of a patient with jargon aphasia, quoted by Butterworth (1985)

Experimenter: What does 'strike while the iron is hot' mean?
Patient: Better to be good and to Post Office and to Pillar Box and to distribution to mail and survey and headmaster. Southern Railways very good and London and Scotland.

Example 6.9. Three types of error shown by patients with jargon aphasia (Butterworth, 1985)

1) The patient repeats the phonological string he has just produced, even though this is no longer appropriate. This results in repetitions of words
You get the one one, and the smaller one, rather larger smaller.

2) The patient manages to access the phonology of a word other than the one required. This results in the production of new, but inappropriate words.
But I seem to table you correctly, sir.

3) The patient fails to access the phonology of any word and produces nonsense strings of phonology. This leads to the production of neologisms.
I'm not very happy, doctor. I've not norter with the verker.

The speech of patients with jargon aphasia has been studied in detail by Brian Butterworth (1985). Butterworth demonstrated that, as with many other types of aphasia, jargon aphasia is the result of a word-finding difficulty. Here again, the difficulty is principally one of generating the appropriate phonology for the required word. However, and this is the critical difference from other kinds of aphasia, patients with jargon aphasia are not content to say nothing. They say something even though they cannot generate the phonology they need. In addition they cannot monitor their own output effectively or edit out errors prior to output. These problems lead to the three main types of error shown in Example 6.9

These errors are different from those produced by schizophrenic patients, because they are caused by problems in accessing phonology. Schizophrenic patients have no difficulty in generating phonology, but they do have problems generating higher level aspects of speech, such as ideas. If we replace difficulties in generating phonology with difficulties in generating ideas, the three error types shown by patients with jargon aphasia parallel those shown by schizophrenic patients. The schizophrenic patient with poverty of content and/or incoherence shows the same form of error as the patient with jargon aphasia. The patient:

1. Repeats ideas just produced when these are no longer appropriate. This results in repetition of words and ideas—poverty of content.
2. Manages to access an idea, but it is not an appropriate one. This would appear as derailment or tangentiality.

3. Fails to access any idea, and puts together a random sequence of components (words and phrases). This results in incoherence.

On this account, the fundamental deficit associated with schizophrenic speech lies in the initiating and accessing of new ideas in a discourse. This is quite different from the fundamental deficit in jargon aphasia; accessing the phonology necessary to turn a semantic unit into a word. What these two speech disorders have in common are the strategies adopted to overcome the underlying problems. In this respect, both disorders differ from other kinds of aphasia. It is possible that the critical defect that gives rise to this strategy is that, in both disorders, the patients cannot monitor their own intended speech.

McCarthy & Warrington (1990) quote two studies that both concluded that jargon aphasia was associated with damage to the parieto-temporal junction and the arcuate fasciculus: the tract joining Broca's area and Wernicke's area. It is plausible that damage to this tract would impair their ability monitor intended utterances.

Language Abnormalities in Patients with Lesions of the Frontal Cortex

A persistent theme in this book concerns the similarity between schizophrenic behaviour and that shown by patients with frontal lobe lesions. There have been several recent studies of language in patients with frontal lobe lesions. The language abnormalities shown by these patients bear a striking similarity to those shown by schizophrenic patients. The literature that permits this comparison to be made has been most usefully reviewed by John McGrath (1991).

In his review, McGrath refers to the work of Alexander and his colleagues (1989) who reached a number of conclusions regarding the effects of lesions to the frontal cortex on language. Lesions in the left cingulate and the supplementary motor area lead to poverty of speech. Both left and right anterior frontal cortex are necessary for the organisation and executive control of language. The right side seems to be particularly concerned with the social and situational control of language. Communication abnormalities in patients with right frontal lesions include "tangentiality, unanticipated changes of topic, socially inappropriate discourse … frankly confabulatory or delusional content in a clear sensorium" (Alexander et al., 1989, p. 684). In other words they talked nonsense even though they were not demented.

Kaczmarek (1987) found that patients with lesions of the dorsolateral prefrontal cortex repeated themselves, used simple sentences and had poverty of speech. In contrast, patients with left orbito-frontal lesions digressed frequently and did not correct their errors.

Others have also concluded that poverty of speech in the form of mutism or a lack of spontaneous speech can be observed after lesions in parts of the frontal cortex. For example, lesions of the anterior cingulate cortex and of the supplementary motor area are associated with poverty of speech and a lack of emotional expression (Damasio & Van Hoesen, 1983). Similar changes can occur after lesions of the basal ganglia (Cancelliere & Kertesz, 1990). It is very likely that all these structures, including prefrontal cortex are part of a functional loop (Alexander et al., 1986). Damage to any part of this loop may result in poverty of action or speech. McGrath suggests that the various defects of language observed in schizophrenia may reflect defects in the various cortical–subcortical loops that project to the prefrontal cortex. These are the same brain systems that are implicated in the other defects of willed action that I have already discussed in Chapter 4.

CONCLUSIONS

In many crucial ways the abnormalities of speech shown by schizophrenic patients resemble their abnormalities in other spheres of action. Schizophrenic patients have difficulty in generating spontaneous ideas in speech, just as they do with other kinds of actions. Also, in speech, just as in other acts, we can observe stereotyped and perseverative behaviour. Incoherent speech, however, is different and calls for additional explanation. Patients do not structure their discourse in such a way that the listener can understand how the various components link together or what the purpose of the communication might be. There are probably a number of different abnormalities underlying this lack of structure. Both poverty and incoherence of speech can be observed in the speech of patients with frontal lobe lesions. Clearly we are concerned with the highest levels of language processing, involved in the planning and execution of discourse. But these are vague terms. What mechanisms underlie these processes and what is the role of the frontal lobes? If planning and executive processes are involved, then abilities in many spheres should be impaired in addition to speech acts. Is there any unifying process that underlies language abnormalities as well as the characteristic signs and symptoms of schizophrenia? In the last chapter, I shall consider just such a unifying scheme.

CHAPTER 7

Schizophrenia as a Disorder of Self-Awareness

EXPLAINING THE SIGNS AND SYMPTOMS OF SCHIZOPHRENIA

My major purpose in writing this book has been to reveal the cognitive processes underlying the various features of schizophrenia. I propose that there are three principal abnormalities, which account for all the major signs and symptoms.

Disorders of Willed Action

Many patients with schizophrenia characteristically show a poverty of action in all spheres: movement, speech, and affect (see Chapter 4). Extreme cases would be described as showing abulia (no will), alogia (no words), and athymia (no feelings). I have suggested that impairment in willed action underlies all these signs. These patients can perform routine acts elicited by environmental stimuli, but have difficulty in producing spontaneous behaviour in the absence of external cues.

However, this problem with willed action can also lead to positive behavioural disorders. In such cases the patient is unable to generate the appropriate behaviour of their own will, and also fails to supress inappropriate behaviour. Recent actions are repeated (perseverations) and responses are made to irrelevant external stimuli, so that action plans cannot be carried through to completion. This leads to incoherent speech and behaviour.

These behaviour patterns: poverty of action, perseveration, and behaviour elicited by irrelevant external stimuli, resemble those seen in patients with frontal lobe lesions. These patients can also show poverty of action, perseverations, and distractible behaviour. Tim Shallice's account of the Supervisory Attentional System (Shallice, 1988) is an attempt to construct a cognitive model in which both these apparently different kinds of behaviour are the result of one and the same deficit in the SAS. The SAS normally modulates the performance of a lower level system that controls the production of routine actions. In the absence of such modulation it is difficult to generate behaviour in situations for which no routine action is appropriate. This difficulty is expressed as a lack of spontaneous, self-willed action (poverty of will). In addition, routine actions will not easily be terminated when they cease to be appropriate (perseveration). Lastly, in the absence of modulation from the SAS, routine actions may be elicited by environmental stimuli when they are inappropriate (distractability, incoherent behaviour).

Summary
Inability to generate spontaneous (willed) acts can lead to:

1. poverty of action (Example 4.1);
2. perseveration (Example 6.2);
3. inappropriate action (Example 6.2);

(see also Table 4.1).

Disorders of Self-monitoring

I propose that many of the experiences classified as first rank symptoms, for example delusions of alien control, can be interpreted as arising from a defect of self-monitoring (see Chapter 5). Patients with these symptoms are no longer aware of the "sense of effort" or the prior intention that normally accompanies a deliberate act. They can only fully monitor their actions on the basis of peripheral feedback, i.e. by observing the actual consequences of their actions after they have been carried out. In the absence of an awareness of their own intentions, patients will experience their actions and thoughts as being caused, not by themselves, but by some alien force. A similar argument can be applied to auditory hallucinations. The patients perceive their own thoughts, subvocal speech, or even vocal speech as emanating, not from their own intentions, but from some source that is not under their control. Patients with positive symptoms have no difficulty in monitoring other kinds of information (e.g. peripheral feedback) to control their behaviour. The difficulty is specific to those actions that they themselves initiate. These patients can still act spontaneously on the basis of willed intentions, unlike those with negative features. However, patients with positive symptoms are no longer aware of these intentions.

Summary
Inability to monitor willed intentions can lead to delusions of alien control, certain auditory hallucinations, thought insertion (see Example 5.1).

Disorders in Monitoring the Intentions of Others

Paranoid delusions and delusions of reference both occur because the patient has made incorrect inferences about the intentions of other people (see Chapter 6). Patients with delusions of reference incorrectly believe that other people are intending to communicate with them. Patients with paranoid delusions believe that other people are intending them harm. Failure to infer the knowledge and intentions of others will also result in certain kinds of incoherent speech because the patients may fail to provide information that would be critical for others to understand what they are talking about. In some cases their inferences (correct or otherwise) about what other people are thinking may be perceived as information coming from an external source, giving rise to third person hallucinations in which voices make comments about the patient.

Summary
Inability to monitor the beliefs and intentions of others leads to delusions of reference, paranoid delusions, certain kinds of incoherence, and third person hallucinations (see Example 5.1).

WHAT IS METAREPRESENTATION?

I have described three classes of schizophrenic features and the different cognitive mechanisms that might underlie these features. I will now attempt to show that these three mechanisms are all special cases of a more general mechanism. If such a general mechanism exists then it will provide a single underlying cognitive framework for describing all the features of schizophrenia. If we can demonstrate a unity at the level of cognitive processes, then is it more reasonable to believe that there is a single entity underlying schizophrenia, despite its many surface manifestations. In this chapter, I shall suggest that all the cognitive abnormalities underlying the signs and symptoms of schizophrenia are reflections of a defect in a mechanism that is fundamental to conscious experience. This mechanism has many labels. I shall use the term metarepresentation.

Disorders of Consciousness in Schizophrenia

The ability to reflect upon how we represent the world and our thoughts, is the most striking feature of our conscious experience. While thinking what to write at this point, I have been staring straight out of the window. In front of me are many trees. When I become conscious of this activity, what I become conscious of is "me looking at trees". This is the critical feature of conscious awareness. It is not representing "a tree", because I was looking at the tree for some time without being aware of it. It is representing "me looking at a tree". This is representation of a representation and, hence, metarepresentation. I propose that meta-representation is the crucial mechanism that underlies this self-awareness. Self-awareness cannot occur without meta-representation. It follows that people who have difficulty with meta-representation must also have an abnormal state of self-awareness. They should certainly have great difficulty in describing their inner experiences. People without metarepresentation should be entirely unable to describe their inner experiences.

Russel Hurlburt (1990) has investigated this ability in an intensive study of a small number of patients with schizophrenia. Hurlburt has developed a method that requires subjects to describe, in as much detail as possible, their inner experiences at the instant that a randomly programmed "beeper" gives a signal. He found three schizophrenic patients in remission who could carry out this task. However, the task was not easy for them. They experienced difficulty in switching to the introspective mode at the beginning of each observation period. In addition some features of their inner experience were recognised by the patients to be abnormal ("goofed up" was the expression used). For example, the mental image of an object present in the room was sometimes altered in trivial ways. For example:

> Jennifer's recreations of the physical world contained particular details
> that were slightly modified from the external reality she was viewing or
> could have been viewing if she had turned her attention to it ... Jennifer
> was sitting at a living room table, smoking a cigarette. At the moment

of the beep, she was idly gazing at the blue wall across from her and behind the table, but paying no attention to an image of Joe, one of the other residents, who was sitting on the opposite side of the table. Jennifer could have been looking at the real Joe; at the moment of the beep, however she was seeing an imaginal recreation of him instead ... Jennifer's image of Joe was viewed slightly up and to her front right, in the same place where he was sitting in reality, although she was not looking at him at the time. In the image of Joe, Jennifer could see he was wearing a Walkman portable radio, holding a blue glass in one hand and a lit cigarette in the other. This image accurately portrayed the physical Joe sitting across from her, except that the real Joe was holding a yellow glass, not a blue one.

All three of Hurlburt's schizophrenic patients described these "goofed up" images. Such images were never described by his other subjects, including those with anxiety and depression. Two patients, who were studied while they were floridly ill, were unable to describe their inner experiences at all. Further such direct explorations of the nature of conscious experience in schizophrenia would be of considerable interest.

I have previously suggested that a disorder of consciousness might underlie the signs and symptoms of schizophrenia (Frith, 1979). Then, I proposed that there was a defective filter, which allowed normally unconscious processes to reach awareness. This account explained some aspects of language disorder and also the difficulty patients have with selecting the few relevant stimuli from the many irrelevant ones with which we are all bombarded. A major flaw in this account was the implicit assumption that only conscious processes cause behaviour. I had observed that schizophrenic behaviour seemed excessively influenced by processes that are normally unconscious. I wrongly concluded that these processes had therefore become conscious. A more plausible account of these phenomena is that the greater influence of unconscious processes occurs because of a lack of control from higher level conscious processes (i.e. the supervisory attentional system) which have ceased to function. Both accounts propose an imbalance between high and low level processes with low level processes having a greater preponderance than normal in their effects on the experience and behaviour of schizophrenic patients.

Metarepresentation in Autism

A clue to the nature of this unifying mechanism is provided by the case of early childhood autism. The signs of childhood autism have many similarities with those of schizophrenia. Social withdrawal, stereotyped behaviour, and lack of communication are all typical features of childhood autism and of chronic "negative" schizophrenia. Indeed, the term "autism" was originally coined by Bleuler to describe a feature of schizophrenia. Throughout this book I have assumed that we can approach cognitive abnormalities more directly through symptoms than through diagnosis. I think it likely that the same cognitive abnormalities will underlie psychotic symptoms like auditory hallucinations, whichever particular diagnosis has been given to the patient. From this point of view, consideration of the signs of childhood autism must have relevance for our understanding of the cognitive basis of schizophrenia. Recently, Uta Frith (1989) has presented a theory that has considerable success in explaining many of the signs of childhood autism. I shall outline this theory and then consider its implications for schizophrenia.

Wing and Gould (1979) have shown that three key features distinguish autism from other varieties of mental handicap; autistic aloneness, abnormal communication and a lack of pretend play. Subsequently, it has been shown that these three features are caused by a single, underlying cognitive deficit (Frith, Morton, & Leslie, 1991). This deficit is in the mechanism that permits us to have a "theory of mind" (Premack & Woodruff, 1978) or to "mentalise". Both these terms refer to our belief that other people have minds different from our own and also to our ability to infer the beliefs, wishes, and intentions of other people in order to predict their behaviour. It is this capacity to mentalise that is absent or severely impaired in autism.

This inability can explain all the elements of Wing and Gould's triad of impairments. If autistic children cannot mentalise, then they cannot understand the behaviour of their mother when she talks into a banana (pretend play). This behaviour is only explicable if the child can infer the mother's mental state: that she is pretending that the banana is a telephone. Without mentalising, the child's communication will be abnormal because he will not be able take into account the beliefs and knowledge of the person to whom he is speaking (see Chapter 6). Finally, he will be in a world in which people are no different from objects. He will be alone or "autistic" in Bleuler's sense, because he is denied contact with other minds.

This lack of ability to mentalise can be studied experimentally. Without the ability to mentalise it is very difficult to appreciate that others may have beliefs about the world that we know to be false. For example, the "Smarties test" (Perner et al., 1989) can be used to study the ability to predict behaviour on the basis of a false belief (Figure 7.1). The child is shown a large Smarties tube and asked what is inside. The reply is, "Smarties". The experimenter then reveals that actually there is a small pencil inside. The child is then told, "Your friend, Billy, is coming in soon. What will he say is in the tube?" Normal children over the age of four will say, "Smarties" and clearly find the idea a big joke. "Billy will be disappointed". Most autistic children with mental ages higher than four find no joke and reply, "Billy will say there is a pencil in the tube". Once autistic children know something, they infer that everybody else knows it too.

FIG. 7.1   The "Smarties test". Taken from Frith (1989), with kind permission of the publisher, Blackwell, and the artist Axel Scheffler.

Mentalising and Metarepresentation

Alan Leslie (1987) has considered in detail the cognitive mechanisms that would be required in order to be able to mentalise. Leslie was concerned to explain pretend play in normal children. During the first years of life, a child must learn about the properties of objects; for example, that a banana is yellow, curved, nice to eat, but must be peeled first. Then, at around 18 months, the child starts playing games of pretend. When the mother pretends that a banana is a telephone, why does this not hopelessly confuse everything the child has learned about bananas so far?

These problems can be solved if there are two separate mechanisms for representation, which handle different kinds of material. The first mechanism handles primary representations (or first order representations) which concern the physical state of the world. For example, this mechanism would be used to represent bananas and all their properties. Propositions, at this level of representation (this banana is edible) can be true or false. The second mechanism handles metarepresentations (or second order representations) which concern mental states. This mechanism is used to represent the attitude of pretending that a banana is a telephone (I pretend "this banana, it is a telephone"). Concepts of truth or falsity do not apply to the part of this proposition that is in quotes. All mental states—pretence, beliefs, desires—require metarepresentation and must be kept distinct from representations of reality. Thus the metarepresentation of a pretend telephone is decoupled (to use Leslie's terminology) from first order representations of telephones (and bananas). The only way the child can understand what their mother is doing with the banana is to infer that she is pretending. In other words the child has to represent his mother's intentional state: "This banana, it is a telephone". Metarepresentations are needed, not just for pretence, but for any kind of mental state proposition (e.g. "she believes, 'it is raining' "). In this case "it is raining" is a first order representation of the physical world. A state of mind, such as "she believes, 'it is raining'", requires metarepresentation. The belief may, of course, be false. I am using metarepresentation in the same sense as Leslie (1987). As "it is raining" is a representation of the physical world, then representing "she believes 'it is raining' " is a representation of a representation and hence a metarepresentation.

The Role of Development

It is likely that the cognitive defect in autism is present from birth, although not reliably detectable until about the third year (Schopler &

Mesibov, 1988). As a consequence, the whole course of development must be abnormal. There is evidence that a proportion of schizophrenic patients show signs of social abnormalities during childhood (Castle, Wessely, & Murray, submitted). However, in most cases of schizophrenia, development appears to be entirely normal until the first breakdown, typically in the early 20s. My proposal is that people with schizophrenia resemble people with autism in that they too have impairments in the mechanism that enables them to mentalise. However, in most cases, this mechanism was functioning adequately until their first breakdown. Given these very different developmental histories, this defect will be manifest in different ways. The autistic person has never known that other people have minds. The schizophrenic knows well that other people have minds, but has lost the ability to infer the contents of these minds: their beliefs and intentions. They may even lose the ability to reflect on the contents of their own mind. However, they will still have available ritual and behavioural routines for interacting with people, which do not require inferences about mental states.

Why Do We Need to Represent Mental States?

What are the implications of an impaired ability to represent mental states? Obviously interactions with other people will be affected, as we have seen in Chapter 6. The majority of such interactions depend on verbal communication. It is abundantly clear that such communications cannot occur successfully simply on the basis of knowing what the words mean. Words mean different things in different contexts, and the most important context is the beliefs and intentions of the person saying the words (including their beliefs about the beliefs and intentions of the person to whom they are speaking).

There is experimental evidence that most autistic children are unable to "read" the mental states of others. This lack of a specific ability can explain, rather precisely, much of the abnormal behaviour of autistic children; their lack of pretend play, their impaired social interactions, and their problems with the "pragmatic" aspects of language. In many ways the behaviour of people with autism resembles that of patients with negative schizophrenia. Such patients show a version of Wing's triad: stereotyped behaviour, social withdrawal, and poor language (both in terms of restricted grammar and impaired pragmatics). However, I shall suggest that it is schizophrenic patients with certain positive symptoms, such as paranoid delusions and delusions of reference, who have difficulty inferring correctly the mental states of others. Autistic children, by definition, do not have such positive symptoms, because the presence of hallucinations and delusions is an exclusion criterion for autism in most diagnostic schemes.

Thus, if I am to argue that there is a common cognitive deficit underlying schizophrenia and autism, then there are two major discrepancies that have to be resolved. First, the negative features of schizophrenia resemble those of autism, but I have explained them in terms of a defect of willed action rather than a lack of mentalising ability. Second, I explain some of the positive symptoms of schizophrenia in terms of an impairment in mentalising, while autistic children, who do have problems with mentalising, do not have such positive symptoms. This second discrepancy can be resolved if we take into account the fact that autism and schizophrenia have markedly different ages of onset. The majority of autistic children fail to develop mentalising abilities. They are unaware that other people have different beliefs and intentions from themselves. Even if they manage, with much effort and after a long time, to learn this surprising fact, they will only be able to infer the mental states of others with difficulty and in the simpler cases (Frith, Morton & Leslie, 1991). As a consequence they cannot develop delusions about the intentions of others. Furthermore, they will know, over a lifetime of experience, that their inferences are likely to be wrong and will therefore be ready to accept the assurance of others as to the true state of affairs.

In contrast, schizophrenic patients know well from past experience that it is useful and easy to infer the mental states of others. They will go on doing this even when the mechanism no longer works properly. For the first 20 years or so of life the schizophrenic has handled "theory of mind" problems with ease. Inferring mental states has become routine in many situations and achieved the status of a direct perception. If such a system goes wrong, then the patient will continue to "feel" and "know" the truth of such experiences and will not easily accept correction.

The situation with regard to the first discrepancy is more problematic. Resolution may be achieved at a theoretical level if we can show that defects of will and defects in inferring the mental states of others reflect a similar cognitive deficit. In his book on the development of the "representational mind", Joseph Perner (1991) has presented precisely this argument in relation to a child's knowledge about its own goals.

Knowing About Goals

According to Perner, below the age of two years, children can demonstrate goal-directed behaviour. Goal-directed behaviour differs from stimulus-elicited behaviour (e.g. stopping when the light is red), in that children must have information about the goal to compare with information about what they have achieved so far. With such information children can continuously modify their behaviour until the goal is reached. BUT young children do not know that they have a goal. This is the critical distinction: there is information about a goal and knowledge that I have a goal. This latter kind of knowledge is an example of metarepresentation (second order representation). The type of knowledge available to the child is revealed when "unexpected" results occur, as might be the case in a reversal learning task. The child learns that a sweet is always in the red box, and never in the blue one. The child has a representation of the desired outcome—finding a sweet—and modifies his/her behaviour until this is achieved quickly on each trial by opening the red box. Then the reversal is introduced. The sweet is now consistently placed in the blue box. Without metarepresentation the child's behaviour will slowly change until the new appropriate response becomes habitual. Such a child is not surprised by the reversal (though he may be angered or frustrated by it). The child is not aware of a goal, or that a particular response normally achieves that goal and, as a consequence, shows a brand of stereotyped, perseverative behaviour that Piaget (1936/1953) called "reactions circulaires". Children over the age of two, who are aware of a goal, also know when they unexpectedly fail to achieve that goal. They will show surprise and will abandon the previously successful behaviour. Such a child will not show stereotyped, perseverative behaviour.

This formulation of developmental progress has much in common with Shallice's two systems, which he labels "contention scheduling" and the "supervisory attentional system". Information about goals is contained in the various routines, which are controlled by contention scheduling. Knowledge about this information is available only in the SAS. My main concern in this chapter is to show that these defects, and others, stem from abnormalities of metarepresentation. Just as in the case of awareness of goals, which I have just discussed, most of the experimental work on metarepresentation comes from developmental psychology.

Knowing About our own Intentions

According to Perner, even after children have become aware of goals, they still do not know that they have intentions. Below the age of four years, children do not know whether they have achieved something by accident or by design. Such children do not know whether they chose the correct box (the one with the sweet in) by a lucky guess or because they knew which was the correct box (Perner, 1991). This lack of awareness of intentions applies even to simple movements, as in the experiment on knee jerks described by Shultz, Wells, and Sarda (1980, experiment 2). In this experiment, three-year-olds were unable to differentiate between intentional movements of their leg and a reflex knee jerk elicited by the experimenter. Only at five years did children report that the knee jerk had not been intended. Without this awareness of their own intentions children are not fully conscious of the control they have over their own actions and will experience "magical" control of and by the environment instead. For example, children may believe that cutting up a photograph may harm the person depicted. This magical control is like that of the deluded patient who told me that he got sunburn because other people were lying under sunray lamps and thinking about him. Awareness of our own intentions is also an example of metarepresentation and one of the most important aspects of self-awareness. Once this awareness has been achieved the child can cope with the reversal task much more efficiently. When the reversal occurs the child is not only aware that the goal has not been reached, but is also aware of the intention that led to this failure. They can therefore suppress this inappropriate action and find the new correct action more rapidly.

Knowing About the Intentions of Others

The ability to take into account the intentions and beliefs of other people has been extensively studied by developmental psychologists in recent years (Astington & Gopnik, 1991). This ability, which is crucial for the development of a "theory of mind", has been found lacking in children with autism (Baron-Cohen, Leslie, & Frith, 1985). Without this ability the autistic child cannot handle the possibility that another person may have a different belief. Such a child is incapable of deception or deliberate lying and cannot easily correct errors of communication when such corrections depend upon inferring the beliefs and intentions of others. Here again this ability depends upon metarepresentation (second order representation); knowledge about other people's knowledge.

METAREPRESENTATION AND SCHIZOPHRENIA

On the basis of studies in child development, I have outlined three areas of self consciousness in which metarepresentation (second order representation) plays a key role: awareness of our own goals, awareness of our own intentions, and awareness of other people's intentions. These areas correspond to the the three types of cognitive impairment underlying the signs and symptoms of schizophrenia: (1) without awareness of goals there is poverty of will. This leads to negative and positive behavioural abnormalities; (2) without awareness of intentions there is lack of high level self-monitoring. This leads to abnormalities in the experience of action; (3) with faulty awareness of the intentions of others there are delusions of persecution and delusions of reference. These relationships between defects of awareness and signs and symptoms are shown in Table 7.1.

Trying to Use Lost Abilities

The failure of metarepresentation associated with adult schizophrenia may well be qualitatively different from that associated with childhood autism. The autistic child does not try to infer the mental states of others. In contrast, adult schizophrenic patients, because their early development has been relatively normal, will continue to make inferences about the mental states of others, but will often get these wrong. They will "see" intentions to communicate when none are there (delusions of reference). They may start to believe that people are deliberately behaving in such a way as to disguise their intentions. They will deduce that there is a general conspiracy against them and that people's intentions towards them are evil (paranoid delusions). They still know all about the value of deception. Thus they will try to deceive, and think that others are deceiving them. As they do not correctly infer the beliefs of the person they are trying to deceive their attempts are likely to be easily detected. On the other hand they will not be persuaded that they are incorrect in their belief that others are deceiving them.

Experiences in the Wrong Domain

Representing mental states (metarepresentation) is completely different from representing physical states (primary representation). These states belong to different domains. It would be wrong, for instance, to think that primary representation concerned knowledge like "bananas are yellow", while metarepresentation concerned knowledge like "John is sad". In fact, both of these are examples of primary representation. In contrast, metarepresentation, in the sense in which I use this term, is concerned with knowledge like "Mary believes 'John is sad' " or "Mary believes 'bananas are yellow' ". Thus metarepresentation is concerned with knowledge about representations. This knowledge will have two components, the form of the representation and its content. For example "I know 'X' ", "Mary believes

'X' ", "I intend 'X' ", all have different forms, but the same content (X). I propose that in some schizophrenic patients metarepresentation fails in such a way that the patient remains aware only of the content of these propositions. Thus, I (Chris) might infer about my friend Eve the proposition, "Eve believes 'Chris drinks too much' ". If my mechanism for metarepresentation failed, then, when I thought about Eve, the free floating notion "Chris drinks too much" might enter my awareness. If I described this experience it would be called a third person hallucination. As is shown in the third column of Table 7.1, many positive, first rank symptoms can be explained in this way.

Self-awareness depends on the ability to represent propositions like "My boss wants of me, 'You must be on time' " (metarepresentation). The content of this proposition is "You must be on time". In schizophrenia the ability to represent such propositions is defective in the various ways shown in Table 7.1

Such experiences depend upon metarepresentations having been formed correctly in the past. If a person has never formed a metarepresentation, then the abnormal experience of the free floating content of such a proposition cannot occur. A person cannot stand in the wrong functional relationship to a proposition if that proposition has never been formed. It follows from this argument that people (such as those with autism) who have not developed the ability to mentalise cannot experience first rank symptoms. It also follows that those rare people with autism who do eventually manage to perform sophisticated theory of mind tasks (Happé, 1991) are potentially able to experience first rank symptoms. Indeed there are a few reports of such cases (Petty et al., 1984; Volkmar, Cohen, & Paul, 1986; Watkins, Asarnow, & Tanguay, 1988).

METAREPRESENTATION AND THE BRAIN

The concept of metarepresentation is sufficiently new that there are not yet any direct investigations of the brain systems involved in this ability either in neurological patients or in experimental lesion studies in animals. Furthermore, metarepresentation is, of its nature, different from other kinds of representation. Much of neuropsychology has been concerned with the location of representations in the brain. Thus we know something about where faces are represented in the brain (Perret et al., 1986), where words are represented (McCarthy & Warrington, 1990) and where movements are represented (Kolb & Wishaw, 1983). I could have given many other examples. I think it very unlikely that metarepresentation will have a location in this way. In Alan Leslie's notation metarepresentation is represented as a proposition of the form,

TABLE 7.1

The signs and symptoms of schizophrenia described as defects of self-awareness

Level of awareness	Level of defect		
	Impaired content	Detached content	No content
Own goals *I must "go to work"*	*I must "become the boss'"* Grandiose ability Grandiose identity Delusion of depersonalisation	*"Go to work"* Delusions of control Thought echo Voices commenting	*(No goals)* Lack of will Stereotyped behaviour Catatonia
Own intentions *I intend to "catch the bus'"*	*I intend to "catch the plane'"* Grandiose ideas Depersonalisation	*"catch the bus"* Delusions of control Thought insertion Thought broadcast Voices commenting	*(No intentions)* Thought withdrawal Poverty of action Poverty of thought Loss of affect
Others' intentions *My boss wants of me "you must be on time"*	*My boss wants of me "you must die"* Delusions of reference Delusions of persecution Derealisation	*"you must be on time"* Voices talking to the patient Voices talking about the patient	*(No mentalizing)* Social withdrawal Autism

for example, "I intend, 'to get up' ". This proposition has a content ('get up') and a functional relationship to that content ("I intend to"). I think it likely that, if such a proposition is instantiated in the brain, then there must be at least two components that similarly have a special relationship. One component will be the content of the proposition and the other will concern the special function of the proposition. It seems reasonable to assume that the content of the proposition can be equated with simple, primary representations of information in the brain. Thus, the content of the proposition, "I intend to, 'get up' ", will be located in the part of the brain concerned with the representation of movement. To achieve representation of the whole proposition ("I intend to 'get up' ") an additional brain system will be interacting with that part of the brain representing the content. Thus metarepresentation will be found to involve a distributed brain system, part of which is defined by the content of the relevant proposition.

Evidence from Studies of Social Cognition

While there have been no direct studies of metarepresentation, there have been many studies of abilities likely to require metarepresentation. I have emphasised three principal contents (domains) for metarepresentation (or self-awareness): the mental states of others, the mental states of the self, and goals (desired outcomes in the real world). Brothers (1990) has proposed that there is a specific brain system (a separable module) concerned with "social cognition". Brothers defines the end result of social cognition as the "accurate perception of the dispositions and intentions of other individuals". He does not, however, consider the special problem raised by the representation of mental states. Brothers identifies three brain areas that are important for social cognition.

The amygdala is concerned with the reward values of objects: whether they are nice or nasty. This role is extended to feelings and emotions. Largely on the basis of human stimulation studies by Gloor (1986), Brothers suggests that the amygdala also stores information about a very wide range of "affects", which reflect subtle nuances in the feelings invoked by different social situations.

The superior temporal sulcus is involved with many different aspects of the faces of conspecifics. This includes facial expression (Perrett et al., 1986) and direction of gaze (Campbell et al., 1990), both of which are crucial information for social cognition.

The orbital-frontal cortex seems to be involved in social interactions. Patient EVR (Eslinger & Damasio, 1985), who has an extensive orbito-frontal lesion, has intact knowledge about social situations, but has lost the ability to behave appropriately in such situations. "Although there were no impairments on any neuropsychological tests and his intelligence is above average, his inability to draw correct conclusions about the motivations of those around him has led him into associations with people of doubtful character, resulting in his bankruptcy." (Brothers, 1990).

Lesions of this area in monkeys also produce social defects. Raleigh & Stelkis (1981) found that orbito-frontal lesions in vervet monkeys living in social groups, resulted in less grooming, less huddling, and greater likelihood of being far from other animals. Huddling and spatial relationships were not altered by temporal lesions. Franzen and Myers (1973) found that lesions of prefrontal or of anterior temporal cortex led to decreased frequencies of various social interactions. In contrast, social deficits were not produced by lesions in cingulate cortex or visual association cortex. It remains to be seen whether these social deficits can be explained as secondary consequences of the cognitive deficits known to follow frontal lesions.

Kirkpatrick and Buchanan (1990) were concerned to delineate a putative neural circuit underlying the enduring negative features of schizophrenia (diminished social drive, poverty of speech, and blunting of affect). Reviewing evidence from animal studies and neurological patients, which overlaps with that considered by Brothers, they suggest that there is a specific neural circuit underlying "social affiliation". This circuit includes the amygdala and the prefrontal cortex, either dorso-lateral or orbito-frontal. Kirkpatrick and Buchanan consider that supplementary motor area, cingulate cortex, and anterior temporal pole may also be involved, although the evidence is not strong.

If we consider this evidence in terms of metarepresentation, then we are led to a slightly different interpretation. Many of the brain areas considered by Brothers to be important for social cognition, are concerned with primary representations: direction of gaze, facial expression, subtypes of affect. Of course, such information is needed for making inferences about the mental states of others. However, I suggest that these brain areas do not, on their own, provide a mechanism for representing the mental states of others. Thus, cells in the temporal cortex might signal "an embarrassed face". By interacting with other brain areas, this could be the basis of a propositions such as, "She feels, 'I am embarrassed' ". I would therefore propose that this brain system for social cognition can be mapped onto metarepresentation as follows: temporal cortex and amygdala provide crucial information for the content of propositions, while full metarepresentation requires that these structures are interacting with frontal cortex. Similar cortico–cortical interactions underlie much simpler propositions outside the social domain. For example, learning that red objects are rewarded ("this red object is nice") requires an intact temporal lobe. Learning a conditional task in which the red object is a cue (this red object means 'go left' ") requires intact frontal and temporal cortex (Gaffan & Harrison, 1988; Ridley & Baker, 1991).

Brain Systems Underlying Willed Action

William James (1890) defined willed action as an action that we consciously and deliberately choose from among a number of possibilities. Awareness of such a choice depends upon meta-representation. When carrying out a willed action we are aware of the goal and of the method we have chosen to attain it. I have already discussed Tim Shallice's mechanism for achieving willed actions and how these may usefully be contrasted with stimulus-driven actions. Shallice's SAS may be conceived of as a system that represents the goal-directed actions carried out at the lower level of primary (or first order) representation. I have discussed in Chapter 4 the evidence that willed actions (actions carried out in the absence of stimuli) involve a brain system in which prefrontal cortex plays a vital part and in which SMA and the basal ganglia are also involved (see Figure 4.3).

With my colleagues at the MRC Cyclotron Unit, I have recently completed a preliminary study of normal volunteers in which positron emission tomography (PET) was used to study brain function while subjects performed willed actions (in James' sense) in two different domains: selecting a finger movement and selecting a word (Frith et al., 1991a). Willed action in both these domains was associated with an increase in blood flow (and hence neural activity) in dorso-lateral prefrontal cortex (Brodmann areas 9 and 46). This result is consistent with neuropsychological evidence from patients with frontal lesions. In addition we observed decreases in blood flow (and hence reduction in neural activity) in regions specific to the two response domains. For word selection these areas were at the back of superior temporal cortex encompassing Wernicke's area. This area is a strong candidate for the location of representations of auditory word forms. For finger selection there were decreases in blood flow in sensori-motor cortex in the position on the sensori-motor strip where finger movement and sensation is located and also at the end of the angular gyrus (area 39) where lesions are found to produce finger agnosia (Mazzoni et al., 1990), i.e. an area that is likely to be involved in distinguishing one finger from another. Thus, in both tasks, brain areas are implicated that are likely to store the primary representations for the responses the subjects had to generate. In other words, they store what becomes the content of propositions, such as "I intend to move, 'my first finger' " or "I intend to say, 'the word wolf' ".

Thus, for willed actions as well as social cognition, the appropriate metarepresentation may depend upon an interaction between prefrontal cortex and those parts of the brain concerned with the primary representations that are the content of the relevant proposition. It remains to be seen whether the different functional relationships of these propositions (e.g. intend, believe, know, etc.) correspond to different locations in prefrontal cortex.

Experimental Studies of Self-awareness in Animals?

None of the studies reviewed above prove that defects of self-awareness can be caused by lesions in particular brain areas. In order to make causal statements, experimental studies in animals will be required. Obviously it is not possible to study features of schizophrenia, such as delusions and hallucinations, in animals. Such features can only be studied via the introspective reports of the subjects. I have argued previously that one of the advantages of defining features like hallucinations in terms of cognitive processes is that it might be possible to study these same processes in animals. I have now suggested that the most appropriate cognitive process is metarepresentation. As the central feature of metarepresentation is that it concerns the reflexive nature of consciousness, this might seem as difficult to study in animals as hallucinations. This conclusion is unduly pessimistic, however. Certainly we cannot study metarepresentation in animals using introspection, but we can study those behaviours that critically depend upon metarepresentation. The question becomes, do animals show such behaviours? That animals can represent the mental states of others remains deeply controversial. Byrne and Whiten (1988) have presented a number of observational studies suggesting that higher primates such as baboons and chimpanzees show evidence of deliberate deceit, which is the acid test of the ability to represent the mental states of others. This ability to deceive has never been brought under experimental control in animal studies, although it has proved possible in studies of young children. Observations in animals are always open to other interpretations. In particular, there is always the danger of anthropomorphism, whereby the "theory of mind" is in the observer and not in the animal observed. In lower primates it is very likely that representation of the mental states of others is not possible. This is certainly the conclusion reached by Cheney and Seyfarth (1990) after an intensive study of the vervet monkey. These monkeys show extensive and complex social interactions, but do not appear to have the ability to deceive.

Representing the mental states of others is the most complex form of metarepresentation. If primates below man very nearly reach this level, then it is more than likely that they are capable of less advanced forms, for example representing their own intentions and being aware of their own goals. In Chapter 5, I described an experiment showing that rats can monitor their own actions (Beninger et al., 1974). This result suggests that these animals have some kind of self-awareness. In recent years there have been many attempts to devise tasks that tap different aspects of learning and memory in rats and monkeys (see Ridley & Baker, 1991 for a review of this literature). Episodic memory is of particular interest as it is specifically impaired in amnesic patients (Ridley & Baker, 1991). Perner (1991) considers that episodic memory depends upon metarepresentation because such memories require us to be aware of the source of the memory ("I remember myself seeing it"). Ridley and Baker (1991) have argued that learning tasks used with monkeys (and rats) can be divided into those requiring primary and secondary representation. In particular they suggest that tasks involving memory of what happened on a unique previous trial require a form of episodic memory that may depend upon secondary representation. A somewhat similar position is taken by Goldman-Rakic (1987) in her account of delayed response learning, which also depends upon memory of a unique previous trial. She suggests that behaviour in this task depends upon "representational memory". Gaffan (1987) suggests that tasks of this sort depend on "personal memory" ("recollection of one's personal history in relation to events"). In many cases it has been shown that successful performance of these tasks, which require some kind of secondary or inner representation, depends upon two interconnected brain regions remaining intact. For example, Goldman-Rakic (1987) proposes that visual–spatial problems involve parietal–prefrontal connections, while problems that entail the use of episodic memory involve limbic–prefrontal connections. Anatomical studies have shown that there are many reciprocal connections between prefrontal cortex and various areas of association cortex (Figure 7.2). These interconnections would permit prefrontal cortex to have the special role in the mechanism of metarepresentation that I have already discussed. Deakin et al. (1989) have found some evidence for neurochemical abnormalities in the brains of schizophrenic patients in areas of temporal and frontal cortex connected by the uncinate fasciculus. Hyde, Ziegler, & Weinberger (in press) have observed that patients with metachromatic leucodystrophy (MLD) frequently have auditory hallucinations and bizarre delusions in the early stages of the disease. At this stage, MLD is associated with demyelination of frontal white matter, particularly periventricular frontal white matter and corpus callosum. Thus there is some evidence that abnormalities in the connections between frontal cortex and other parts of the brain are associated with psychotic symptoms.

It is clear that a number of tasks have already been developed which can be performed by animals and which have properties requiring cognitive processes that have resemblances to metarepresentation. Studies of the effects of lesions on these tasks have highlighted distributed brain systems similar to those which I have suggested might underlie the signs and symptoms of schizophrenia. In the next few years there will almost certainly be animal studies aimed more directly at understanding metarepresentation. In addition, new developments in functional brain imaging will allow us to map the relevant brain systems in humans also (Frith, 1991a).

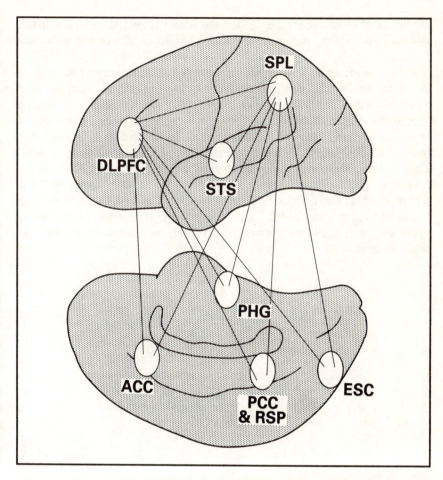

FIG. 7.2 Lateral and medial views of the human brain showing interconnections with prefrontal cortex (area 46) after Goldman-Rakic (1987). Abbreviations: ACC, anterior cingulate cortex; DLFPC, dorsolateral prefrontal cortex; ESC, extra-striate cortex; PHG, parahippocampal gyrus; PCC, posterior cingulate cortex; RSP, retrosplenal cortex; STS, superior temporal sulcus.

CONCLUSIONS

In this chapter I have proposed a, doubtless over-inclusive, framework for linking the signs and symptoms of schizophrenia to abnormal brain function in terms of a single cognitive process: metarepresentation. I have suggested how specific features of schizophrenia might arise from specific abnormalities in metarepresentation. This is the cognitive mechanism that enables us to be aware of our goals, our intentions, and the intentions of other people. I have also suggested how the brain systems underlying metarepresentation might be studied in man and animals.

My theory may be wrong, but I believe that the approach I have used is the most fruitful for understanding the signs and symptoms of schizophrenia. The advantages of this approach are, first, that a framework for understanding the relationships between the various signs and symptoms of schizophrenia is provided. Second, this framework links signs and symptoms with specific cognitive processes. Third, the framework provides criteria for identifying aspects of brain function and animal behaviour relevant to the symptoms of schizophrenia. The framework I have used is, of course, that of cognitive neuropsychology in which specification of cognitive mechanisms provides the crucial link between behaviour, conscious experience and brain systems.

Appendices

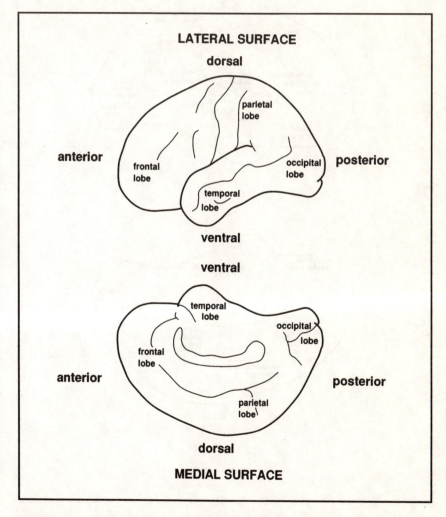

APPENDIX 1. Lateral and medial views of the left hemisphere of the human brain.

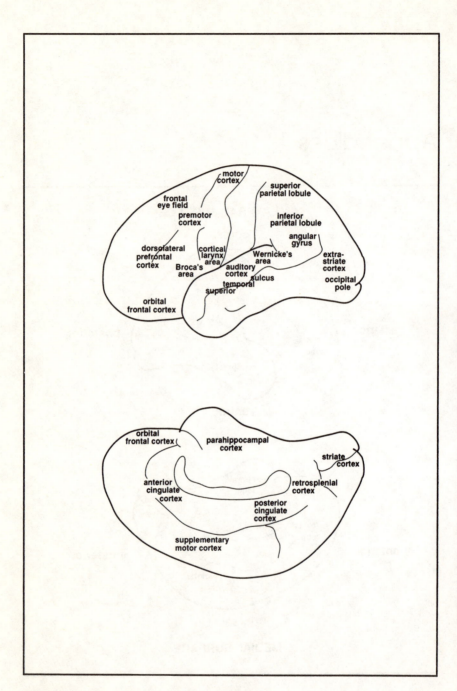

APPENDIX 2. Location of principal cortical areas.

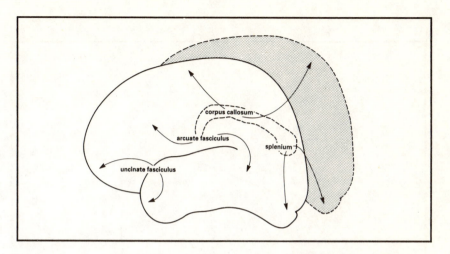

APPENDIX 3. The major connecting pathways within and between hemispheres.

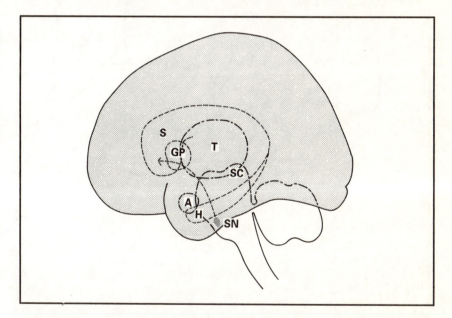

APPENDIX 4. Lateral view through the brain showing the major internal structures. A, amygdala; GP, globus pallidus; H, hippocampus; S, striatum; SC, superior colliculus; SN, substantia nigra (showing dopamine projection to the striatum); T, thalamus. The major components of the striatum are the caudate and the putamen. The major components of the basal ganglia are the striatum and the globus pallidus. The major components of the limbic system are the amygdala, the hippocampus, the parahippocampal gyrus and the cingulate gyrus.

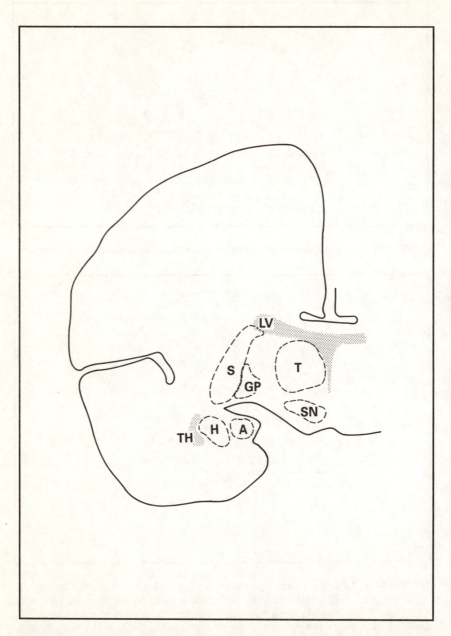

APPENDIX 5. Coronal cross-section through one hemisphere showing the major internal structures. This slice is about 1 cm anterior to that shown in Figure 2.3. A, amgydala; GP, globus pallidus; H, hippocampus; LV, body of the lateral ventricle; S, striatum; SN, substantia nigra; T, thalamus; TH, temporal horn of the lateral ventricle.

References

Ackner, B., Harris, A., & Oldham, A.J. (1957). Insulin treatment of schizophrenia: a controlled study. *Lancet, i,* 607–611.

Albert, E. (1987). On organically based hallucinatory-delusional psychoses. *Psychopathology, 20,* 144–154.

Alexander, G.E., DeLong, M., & Strick, P.E. (1986). Parallel organisation of functionally segregated circuits linking basal ganglia and cortex. *Annual Review of Neuroscience, 9,* 357–381.

Alexander, M.P., Stuss, D.T., & Benson, D.F. (1979). Capgras' syndrome: A reduplicative phenomenon. *Neurology, 29,* 334–339.

Alexander, M.P., Benson, D.F., & Stuss, D.T. (1989). Frontal lobes and language. *Brain and Language, 37,* 656–691.

Allen, H.A. (1983). Do positive and negative language symptom subtypes of schizophrenia show qualitative differences in language production? *Psychological Medicine, 13,* 787–797.

Allen, H.A. (1984). Positive and negative symptoms and the thematic organisation of schizophrenic speech. *British Journal of Psychiatry, 144,* 611–617.

Allen, H.A. (1990). Cognitive processing and its relationship to symptoms and social functioning in schizophrenia. *British Journal of Psychiatry, 156,* 201-203

Allen, H.A., & Frith, C.D. (1983). Selective retrieval and free emission of category exemplars in schizophrenia. *British Journal of Psychology, 74,* 481–490.

Allen, H.A., Liddle, P.F., & Frith, C.D. (submitted) Negative features, retrieval processes and verbal fluency in schizophrenia.

Alpert, M., & Silvers, K. (1970). Perceptual characteristics distinguishing auditory hallucinations in schizophrenia and acute alcoholic psychoses. *American Journal of Psychiatry, 127,* 298–302.

Alzheimer, A. (1907). Über eine eigenartige Erkrankung der Hirnrinde. *Allgemeine Zeitschrift für Psychiatrie, 64*, 146–148.

American Psychiatric Association (1987). *Diagnostic and statistical manual of mental disorders DSM-III-R* (3rd rev. ed.) Washington DC: APA.

Andén, N.E., Carlsson, A., Dahlstrom, A., Fuxe, K., Hillarp, N.A., & Larsson, K. (1964). Demonstration and mapping out of nigro-striatal dopamine neurons. *Life Sciences, 3*, 523–530.

Andreasen, N.C. (1979). Thought, language and communication disorders: 2 Diagnostic significance. *Archives of General Psychiatry, 36*, 1325–1330.

Andreasen, N.C. (1985). *The comprehensive assessment of symptoms and history (CASH).* Iowa City: The University of Iowa Press.

Andreasen, N.C., & Flaum, M. (1991). Schizophrenia: the characteristic symptoms. *Schizophrenia Bulletin, 17*, 27–49.

Andreasen, N.C., Olsen, S.A., Dennert, J.W., & Smith, M.R. (1982). Ventricular enlargement in schizophrenia: relationship to positive and negative symptoms. *American Journal of Psychiatry, 139*, 297–302.

Andreasen, N.C., Hoffman, R.E., & Grove, W.M. (1985). Mapping abnormalities in Language and cognition. In A. Alpert (Ed.) *Controversies in schizophrenia: changes and constancies.* (pp. 199–226). Guilford Press, New York.

Angrist, B., Lee, H.K., & Gershon, S. (1974a). The antagonism of amphetamine induced symptomatology by a neuroleptic. *American Journal of Psychiatry, 131*, 817–819.

Angrist, B., Sathananthan, G., Wilk, S., & Gershon, S. (1974b). Amphetamine psychosis: behavioural and biochemical aspects. *Journal of Psychiatric Research, 11*, 13–23.

Angrist, B., Rotrosen, J., & Gershon, S. (1980). Differential effects of amphetamine and neuroleptics on negative vs positive symptoms in schizophrenia. *Psychopharmacology, 72*, 17–19.

Arndt, S., Alliger, R.J., & Andreasen, N.C. (1991). The distinction of positive and negative symptoms: the failure of a two-dimensional model. *British Journal of Psychiatry, 158*, 317–322.

Astington, J.W., & Gopnik, M. (1991). Theoretical explanations of children's understanding of mind. *British Journal of Developmental Psychology, 9*, 7–31.

Baddeley, A. (1986). *Working memory.* Oxford: Oxford University Press.

Baddeley, A & Lewis, V.J. (1981). Inner active processes in reading: The inner voice, the inner ear and the inner eye. In A. M. Lesgold & C. A. Perfetti (Eds.), *Interactive processes in reading.* (pp. 107–129). Hillsdale, NJ: Lawrence Erlbaum Associates Inc.

Baron-Cohen, S., Leslie, A.M., & Frith, U. (1985). Does the autistic child have a 'theory of mind'? *Cognition, 21*, 37–46.

Baruch, I., Hemsley, D.R., & Gray, J. (1988). Differential performance of acute and chronic schizophrenics in a latent inhibition task. *Journal of Nervous and Mental Disorder, 176*, 598–606.

Basilier, T. (1973). *Hørselstap og egentlig døvhet.* Oslo: Universitetsforlager.

Bauer, R.M. (1984). Autonomic recognition of names and faces in prosopagnosia: a neuropsychological application of the guilty knowledge test. *Neuropsychologia, 22*, 457–469.

Beninger, R.J., Kendall, S.B., & Vanderwolf, C.H. (1974). The ability of rats to discriminate their own behaviours. *Canadian Journal of Psychology, 28*, 79–91.

Benson, D.F. (1990). Psychomotor retardation. *Neuropsychiatry, Neuropsychology, and Behavioral Neurology, 3,* 36–47.

Bentall, R.P. (1990). The syndromes and symptoms of psychosis. In R. P. Bental (Ed.), *Reconstructing schizophrenia.* London: Routledge.

Bentall, R.P., & Slade, P.D. (1985). Reality testing and auditory hallucinations: a signal detection analysis. *British Journal of Clinical Psychology, 24,* 159–169.

Bentall, R.P., Baker, G.A., & Havers, S. (1991a). Reality monitoring and psychotic hallucinations. *British Journal of Clinical Psychology, 30,* 213–222.

Bentall, R.P., Kaney, S., & Dewey, M.E. (1991b). Paranoia and social reasoning: an attribution theory analysis. *British Journal of Clinical Psychology, 30,* 13–23.

Bick, P.A., & Kinsbourne, M. (1987). Auditory hallucinations and subvocal speech in schizophrenic patients. *American Journal of Psychiatry, 144,* 222–225.

Bleuler, E. (1913). Dementia Praecox or the group of schizophrenias. Translated into English, 1987. In J. Cutting & M. Shepherd (Eds.), *The clinical routes of the schizophrenia concept.* Cambridge: Cambridge University Press.

Bodlakova, V., Hemsley, D.R., & Mumford, S.J. (1974). Psychological variables and flattening of affect. *British Journal of Medical Psychology, 47,* 227–234.

Bogerts, B., Meertz, E., & Schonfield-Bausch, R. (1985). Basal ganglia and limbic system pathology in schizophrenia: a morphometric study of brain volume and shrinkage. *Archives of General Psychiatry, 42,* 784–791.

Bowen, D.M., Smith, C.B., White, P., & Davison, A.M. (1976). Neurotransmitter related enzymes and indices of hypoxia in senile dementia and other abiotrophies. *Brain, 99,* 459–495.

Boyle, M. (1990). *Schizophrenia: A scientific delusion?* London: Routledge.

Braff, D., Stone, C., Callaway, E., Geyer, M., Glick, I., & Bali, I. (1978). Presetimulus effects on human startle reflex in normals and schizophrenics. *Psychophysiology, 15,* 339–343.

Braun, C., Bernier, S., Proulx, R., & Cohen, H. (1991). A deficit of primary affective facial expression independent of bucco-facial dyspraxia in chronic schizophrenics. *Cognition and Emotion, 5,* 147–159.

Brennan, J.H., & Hemsley, D.R. (1984). Illusory correlations in paranoid and non-paranoid schizophrenia. *British Journal of Clinical Psychology, 23,* 225–226.

Breslin, N.A., & Weinberger, D.R. (1990). Schizophrenia and the normal functional development of the prefrontal cortex. *Development and Psychopathology, 2,* 409–424.

Brindley, G., & Merton, P.A. (1960). The absence of position sense in the human eye. *Journal of Physiology (Lond.), 153,* 127–130.

Brothers, L. (1990). The social brain: a project for integrating primate behaviour and neurophysiology in a new domain. *Concepts in Neuroscience, 1,* 27–51.

Brown, R., Colter, N., Corsellis, J.A.N., Crow, T.J., Frith, C.D., Jagoe, R., Johnstone, E.C., & Marsh, L. (1986). Post-mortem evidence of structural brain changes in schizophrenia. *Archives of General Psychiatry, 43,* 36–42.

Bruton, C.J., Crow, T.J., Frith, C.D., Johnstone, E.C., Owens, D.G.C., & Roberts, G.W. (1990). Schizophrenia and the brain: A prospective clinico-neuropathological study. *Psychological Medicine, 20,* 285–304.

Burns, A., Jacoby, R., & Levy, R. (1990). Psychiatric phenomena in Alzheimer's disease: II. Disorders of perception. *British Journal of Psychiatry, 157,* 76–81.

Butterworth, B. (1985). Jargon aphasia: Processes and strategies. In S. Newman & R. Epstein (Eds.), *Current perspectives in dysphasia* (pp. 61–97) New York: Churchill Livingstone.

Byrne, R., & Whiten, A. (1988). *Machiavellian intelligence*. Oxford: Oxford University Press.

Campbell, R., Heywood, C.A., Cowey, A., Regard, M., & Landis, T. (1990). Sensitivity to eye gaze in prosopagnosic patients and monkeys with superior temporal sulcus ablation. *Neuropsycholgia, 28,* 1123–1142.

Cancelliere, A.E.B., & Kertesz, A. (1990). Lesion localisation in acquired deficits of emotional expression and comprehension. *Brain and Cognition, 13,* 133–147.

Capgras, J., & Reboul-Lachaux, J. (1923). L'illusion de 'sosies' dans un dlire systmatise chronique. *Bulletin de la Société Clinique de Médecine Mentale, 2,* 6–16.

Carlsson, A., Lindqvist, M., Magnusson, T., & Waldeck, B. (1958). On the presence of 3-hydroxytyramine in the brain. *Science, 127,* 471.

Castle, D.J., Wessely, S., & Murray, R.M. (submitted). Sex and schizophrenia: Effects of diagnostic stringency and association with premorbid variables.

Celesia, G.G., & Barr, A.N. (1970). Psychosis and other psychiatric manifestations of levo-dopa therapy. *Archives of Neurology, 23,* 193–200.

Cheney, D.L., & Seyfarth, R.M. (1990). *How monkeys see the world*. Chicago: Chicago University Press.

Cohen, B.D. (1976). Referent communication in schizophrenia: The perseverative-chaining model. *Annals of the New York Academy of Sciences, 270,* 124–141.

Cohen, B.D. (1978). Referent communication disturbances in schizophrenia. In S. Schwartz (Ed.), *Language and cognition in schizophrenia*. Hillsdale, N.J.: Lawrence Erlbaum Associates Inc.

Cohen, R. (1991). Event related potentials and cognitive dysfunction in schizophrenia. In H. Hafner & W. F. Gattaz (Eds.), *Search for the causes of schizophrenia, vol II*. Berlin: Springer.

Collicutt, J.R., & Hemsley, D.R. (1981). A psychophysical investigation of auditory functioning in schizophrenia. *British Journal of Clinical Psychology, 20,* 199–204.

Connell, P. (1958). *Amphetamine psychosis*. London: Chapman and Hall.

Cools, A.R., Jaspers, R., Schwarz, M., Sontag, K.H., Vrijmoed-de Vries, M., & van den Bercken, J. (1984). Basal ganglia and switching motor programs. In J. S. McKenzie, R. E. Kemm., & L. N. Wilcock (Eds.), *The basal ganglia: Structure and function. Advances in behavioural biology* (vol. 27). New York: Plenum Press.

Cooper, S.J., & Dourish, C.T. (Eds.) (1990). *The neurobiology of behavioural stereotypy*. Oxford: Oxford University Press.

Cotes, P.M., Crow, T.J., Johnstone, E.C., Bartlett, W., & Bourne, R.C. (1978). Neuroendocrine changes in acute schizophrenia as a function of clinical state and neuroleptic medication. *Psychological Medicine, 8,* 657–665.

Critchley, E.M.R., Denmark, J.C., Warren, F., & Wilson, K.A. (1981). Hallucinatory experiences in prelingually profoundly deaf schizophrenics. *British Journal of Psychiatry, 138,* 30–32.

Crow, T.J. (1980). Molecular pathology of schizophrenia: More than one disease process? *British Medical Journal, 280,* 66–68.

Crow, T.J. (1986). The continuum of psychosis and its implication for the structure of the gene. *British Journal of Psychiatry, 149,* 419–429.

Crow, T.J. (1988). Aetiology of psychosis: the way ahead. In P. Bebbington & P. McGuffin (Eds.), *Schizophrenia: The major issues.* Oxford: Heinemann.

Crow, T.J., Cross, A.J., Johnson, J.A., Johnstone, E.C., Joseph, M.H., Owen, F., Owens, D.G.C., & Poulter, M. (1984). Catecholamines and schizophrenia: an assessment of the evidence. In E. Usdin, A. Carlsson, A. Dahlstrom & J. Engel (Eds.), *Catecholamines. Part C: Neuropharmacology and central nervous system - therapeutic aspects.* (pp. 11–20) New York: Liss.

Crow, T.J., Ball, J., Bloom, S.R., Brown, R., Bruton, C.J., Colter, N. Frith, C.D., Johnstone, E.C., Owens, D.G.C., & Roberts, G.W. (1989). Schizophrenia as an anomaly of development of cerebral asymmetry. *Archives of General Psychiatry, 46,* 1145–1150.

Cutting, J. (1985). *The psychology of schizophrenia.* Edinburgh: Churchill Livingstone.

Cutting, J. (1990). *The right cerebral hemisphere and psychiatric disorders.* Oxford: Oxford University Press.

Cutting, J., & Murphy, D. (1990a). Preference for denotative as opposed to connotative meanings in schizophrenics. *Brain and Language, 39,* 459–468.

Cutting, J., & Murphy, D. (1990b). Impaired ability of schizophrenic patients, relative to manics or depresives, to appreciate social knowledge about their culture. *British Journal of Psychiatry, 157,* 355–358.

Damasio, A.R., & Van Hoesen, G.W. (1983). Emotional disturbances associated with focal lesions of the limbic frontal lobe. In K. Heilman, & P. Satz (Eds.), *Neuropsychology of human emotion.* New York: Guilford Press.

Davis, J.M., & Gerver, D.L. (1978). Neuroleptics: Clinical use in psychiatry. In L. L. Iversen, & S. D. Iversen (Eds.), *Handbook of psychopharmacology: (vol. 10). Neuroleptics and schizophrenia.* New York: Plenum Press.

Deakin, J.F.W., Slater, P., Simpson, M.D.C., Gilchrist, A.C., Skan, W.J., Royston, M.C., Reynolds, G.P., & Cross, A.J. (1989). Frontal cortical and left temporal glutamatergic dysfunction in schizophrenia. *Journal of Neurochemistry, 52,* 1781–1786.

Delay, J., & Deniker, P. (1952). Le traitment des psychoses par une methode neurolyptique derive de l'hibernotherapie. In P. Cossa (Ed.), *Congrès de Médicins Aliénistes et Neurologistes de France* (pp. 497–502) Paris: Maisson Editeurs Libraires de l'Academie de Medicine.

Dennett, D.C. (1991). *Consciousness explained.* London: Penguin Press.

De Silva, W.P., & Hemsley, D.R. (1977). The influence of context on language perception in schizophrenia. *British Journal of Social and Clinical Psychology, 16,* 337–345.

Done, D.J., & Frith, C.D. (1984). The effects of context during word perception in schizophrenic patients. *Brain and Language, 23,* 318–336.

Ehringer, H., & Hornykiewicz, O. (1960). Verteilung von Noradrenalin und Dopamin (3-hydroxytyramine) in Gehirn des Menschen und der Verhalten bei Erkrankungen des extrapyramiden Systems. *Klinische Wochenschrift, 38,* 1236–1239.

Ellenbroek, B.A., & Cools, A.R. (1990). Animal models with construct validity for schizophrenia. *Behavioural Pharmacology, 1,* 469–490.

Ellis, H.D., & Young, A.W. (1990). Accounting for delusional misidentifications. *British Journal of Psychiatry, 157,* 239–248.

Eslinger, P.J., & Damasio, A. R. (1985). Severe disturbance of higher cognition after bilateral frontal ablation: patient EVR. *Neurology, 35,* 1731–1741.

Evenden, J.L., & Robbins, T.W. (1983). Increased response switching, perseveration and perseverative switching following D-amphetamine in the rat. *Psychopharmacology, 80,* 67–73.

Farde, L., Wiesel, F., Halldin, C., Stone-Elander, S., & Sedvall, G. (1987). No D2 receptor increase in a PET study of schizophrenia. *Archives of General Psychiatry, 44,* 671–672.

Feinberg, I. (1978). Efference copy and corollary discharge: implications for thinking and its disorders. *Schizophrenia Bulletin, 4,* 636–640.

Feinstein, A., & Ron, M.A. (1990). Psychosis associated with demonstrable brain disease. *Psychological Medicine, 20,* 793–803.

Ferrier, J. (1795). *Medical histories and reflection.* Cadell & Davies: London.

Fodor, J. (1983). *The modularity of mind.* Cambridge, Mass: MIT Press.

Franzen, E.A., & Myers, R.E. (1973). Neural control of social behaviour: prefrontal and anterior temporal cortex. *Neuropsychologia, 11,* 141–157.

Fraser, W., King, K., Thomas, P., & Kendell, R.E. (1986). The diagnosis of schizophrenia by language analysis. *British Journal of Psychiatry, 148,* 275–278.

Frith, C.D. (1979). Consciousness, information processing and schizophrenia. *British Journal of Psychiatry, 134,* 225–235.

Frith, C.D. (1984). Schizophrenia, memory, and anticholinergic drugs. *Journal of Abnormal Psychology, 93,* 339–341.

Frith, C.D. (1987). The positive and negative symptoms of schizophrenia reflect impairments in the perception and initiation of action. *Psychological Medicine, 17,* 631–648.

Frith, C.D. (1991a). Positron emission tomographic studies of frontal lobe function: relevance to psychiatric disease. In *Exploring brain functional anatomy with positron tomography.* CIBA Foundation Symposium 163 (pp. 181–197). Chichester: Wiley.

Frith, C.D., & Allen, H.A. (1988). Language disorders in schizophrenia and their implications for neuropsychology. In P. Bebbington & P. McGuffin (Eds.), *Schizophrenia: the major issues* (pp. 172–186) Heinemann: Oxford.

Frith, C.D., & Done, D.J. (1983). Stereotyped responding by schizophrenic patients on a two-choice guessing task. *Psychological Medicine, 13,* 779–786.

Frith, C.D., & Done, D.J. (1986). Routes to action in reaction time tasks. *Psychological Research, 48,* 169–177.

Frith, C.D., & Done, D.J. (1989). Experiences of alien control in schizophrenia reflect a disorder in the central monitoring of action. *Psychological Medicine, 19,* 359–363.

Frith, C.D., Friston, K.J., Liddle, P.F., & Frackowiak, R.S.J. (1991a). Willed action and the prefrontal cortex in man: A study with PET. *Proceedings of the Royal Society of London, Series B, 244,* 241–246.

Frith, C.D., Leary, J., Cahill, C., & Johnstone, E.C. (1991b). Performance on psychological tests. Demographic and clinical correlates of the results of these tests. In E.C. Johnstone (Ed.), *Disabilities and circumstances of schizophrenic patients: A follow-up study. British Journal of Psychiatry, 159, supplement 13,* 26–29.

Frith, U. (1970). Studies in pattern detection in normal and autistic children. ii. Reproduction and production of colour sequences. *Journal of Experimental Child Psychology, 10*, 120–135.

Frith, U. (1989). *Autism: Explaining the enigma*. Oxford: Blackwell.

Frith, U. (1991b). Asperger and his syndrome. In U. Frith (Ed.), *Autism and Asperger syndrome*. Cambridge: Cambridge University Press.

Frith, U., Morton, J., & Leslie, A.M. (1991c). The cognitive basis of a biological disorder: autism. *Trends in the Neurosciences, 14*, 433–438.

Gaffan, D. (1987). Amnesia, personal memory, and the hippocampus: experimental neuropsychological studies in monkeys. In S. M. Stahl, S. D. Iversen, & E. C. Goodman (Eds.), *Cognitive neurochemistry* (pp. 46–56) Oxford: Oxford University Press.

Gaffan, D., & Harrison, S. (1988). Inferotemporal-frontal disconnection and fornix transection in visuomotor conditional learning in monkeys. *Behavioural Brain Research, 31*, 149–163.

Gallistel, C.R. (1980). *Organisation of action: a new synthesis.* N.J.: Lawrence Erlbaum Associates Inc.

Garety, P.A., Hemsley, D.R., & Wesseley, S. (1991). Reasoning in deluded and paranoid subjects: biases in performance on a probabalistic inferencing task. *Journal of Nervous and Mental Disease, 179*, 194–201.

Gattaz, W.F., Kohlmeyer, K., & Gasser, T. (1991). Computer tomographic studies in schizophrenia. In H. Hafner, & W. F. Gattaz (Eds.), *Search for the causes of schizophrenia* (vol. II). Berlin: Springer.

Gerjuoy, I.R., & Winters, J.O. (1968). Development of lateral and choice sequence preferences. In N.R. Ellis (Ed.), *International review of research in mental retardation* (vol. 3) (pp. 31–63) London: Academic Press.

Gessler, S., Cutting, J., Frith, C.D., & Weinman, J. (1989). Schizophrenic inability to judge facial emotion: a controlled study. *British Journal of Clinical Psychology, 28*, 19–29.

Gloor, P. (1986). Role of the human limbic system in perception, memory and affect. In: B.K. Doane, & K.E.Livingstone (Eds.), *The limbic system: Functional organisation and clinical disorders* (pp. 165-169) New York: Raven Press.

Goldberg, G. (1985). Supplementary motor area structure and function: Review and hypotheses. *The Behavioral and Brain Sciences, 8*, 567–616.

Goldberg, G., Mayer, N.H., & Toglia, J.U. (1981). Medial frontal cortex and the alien hand sign. *Archives of Neurology, 38*, 683–686.

Goldman-Rakic, P. S. (1987). Circuitry of primate prefrontal cortex and regulation of behavior by representational memory. In F. Plum & V. Mountcastle (Eds), *Handbook of physiology: The nervous system.* (American Physiological Society, Bethesda) *5:* (373–417) Baltimore: Williams & Wilkins.

Good, D. (1990). Repair and cooperation in conversation. In P. Luff, N. Gilbert, & D. Frohlich (Eds.), *Computers and conversation* (pp. 133–150) London: Academic Press.

Gottesman, I.I., & Shields, J. (1982). *Schizophrenia: The epigenetic puzzle.* Cambridge: Cambridge University Press.

Gould, L.N. (1949). Auditory hallucinations and subvocal speech. *Journal of Nervous and Mental Disease, 109*, 418–427.

Gray, J., Feldon, J., Rawlins, J., Hemsley, D., & Smith, A. (1990). The neuropsychology of schizophrenia. *Behavioural and Brain Sciences, 14*, 1-84

Green, M.F., & Kinsbourne, M. (1989). Auditory hallucinations in schizophrenia: Does humming help? *Biological Psychiatry, 25,* 633–635.

Green, P., & Preston, M. (1981). Reinforcement of vocal correlates of auditory hallucinations by auditory feedback: A case study. *British Journal of Psychiatry, 139,* 204–208.

Grew, N. (1701). *Cosmologia Sacra: Or a discourse of the universe as it is the creature and kingdom of God.* London: Rogers.

Grice, H.P. (1975). Logic and conversation. In R.Cole & J.Morgan (Eds.), *Syntax and semantics, (vol. 3), Speech acts* (pp. 41–58) New York: Academic Press.

Gross, M.M., Halpert, E., Sabot, L., & Polizos, P. (1963). Hearing disturbances and auditory hallucinations in the acute alcoholic psychoses: I tinnitus, incidence and significance. *Journal of Nervous and Mental Disease, 137,* 455–465.

Gruzelier, J., & Flor-Henry, P., (Eds.) (1979). *Hemisphere asymmetries of function in psychopathology.* Amsterdam: Elsevier/North Holland.

Gruzelier, J., Seymour, K., Wilson, L., Jolley, A., & Hirsch, S. (1988). Impairments of neuropsychological tests of temporohippocampal and frontohippocampal functions and word fluency in remitting schizophrenia and affective disorders. *Archives of General Psychiatry 45,* 623–629.

Gunderson, J.G., & Mosher, L.R. (1975). The cost of schizophrenia. *American Journal of Psychiatry, 132,* 901–906.

Hall, G., & Honey, R. (1989). Contextual effects in conditioning, latent inhibition, and habituation: associative and retrieval functions of contextual cues. *Journal of Experimental Psychology: Animal Behaviour Processes, 15,* 232-241

Happé, F. (1991). *Theory of mind and communication in autism.* Unpublished PhD Thesis, University College London.

Hare, E. (1982). Epidemiology of schizophrenia. In J. K. Wing & L. Wing (Eds.), *Psychoses of uncertain aetiology: Handbook of psychiatry* (vol. 3). Cambridge: Cambridge University Press.

Harrow, M., & Miller, J.G. (1985). Schizophrenic thought disorders and impaired perspective. *Journal of Abnormal Psychology, 89,* 717–727.

Harvey, P.D. (1985). Reality monitoring in mania and schizophrenia. *The Journal of Nervous and Mental Disease, 173,* 67–73.

Hécaen, H., & Albert, M.L. (1975). Disorders of mental function relating to frontal lobe pathology. In D.F. Benson & D. Blumer (Eds.), *Psychiatric aspects of neurological disease.* New York: Grune & Straton.

Helmholtz, H. (1866). *Handbuch der Physiologischen Optik.* Leipzig: Voss.

Hemsley, D.R. (1977). What have cognitive deficits to do with schizophrenic symptoms? *British Journal of Psychiatry, 130,* 167–173.

Hemsley, D.R., & Garety, P.A. (1986). The formation and maintenance of delusions: a Bayesian analysis. *British Journal of Psychiatry, 149,* 51–56.

Hershberger, W., & Misceo, G. (1983). A conditioned weight illusion: Reafference learning without a correlational store. *Perception and Psychophysics, 33,* 391–398.

Hirsch, S. (1982). Medication and physical treatment of schizophrenia. In J.K. Wing & L. Wing (Eds.), *Psychoses of uncertain aetiology: Handbook of Psychiatry 3* (pp. 74–87) Cambridge: Cambridge University Press.

Hoffman, R.E. (1986). Verbal hallucinations and language production processes in schizophrenia. *Behavioral and Brain Sciences, 9,* 503–548.

Hogarty, G.E., Goldberg, S.C., Schooler, N.R., Ulrich, R.F., & Collaborative Study Group. (1974). Drug and sociotherapy in the after care of schizophrenic patients. II. Two-year relapse rates. *Archives of General Psychiatry, 31,* 603–608.

Holst, E. von, & Mittelstaedt, H. (1950). Das Reafferenzprinzip (Wechselwirkungen zwischen Zentralnervensystem und Peripherie). *Naturwissenschaften 37,* 464–476.

Huq, S.F., Garety, P.A., & Hemsley, D.R. (1988). Probabilistic judgements in deluded and non-deluded subjects. *Quarterly Journal of Experimental Psychology, 40A,* 801–812.

Hurlburt, R.T. (1990). *Sampling normal and schizophrenic inner experience.* New York: Plenum Press.

Hyde, T.M., Ziegler, J.C., & Weinberger, D.R. (in press) Psychiatric disturbances in metachromatic leukodystrophy: Insights into the neurobiology of psychosis. *Archives of Neurology.*

James, W. (1890). *The principles of psychology.* London: Macmillan.

Janowsky, J.S., Shimamura, A.P., & Squire, L.R. (1989). Source memory impairment in patients with frontal lobe lesions. *Neuropsychologia, 27,* 1043–1056.

Jaspers, K. (1962). *General psychopathology.* Manchester: Manchester University Press.

Jeste, D.V., & Wyatt, R.J. (1982). *Understanding and treating tardive dyskinesia.* New York: Guilford Press.

Johnson-Laird, P.N. (1982). Thinking as a skill. *Quarterly Journal of Experimental Psychology, 34A,* 1–29.

Johnstone, E.C. (1991). The Harrow (1975–1985) study of the disabilities and circumstances of schizophrenic patients. *British Journal of Psychiatry, 159,* supplement 13, 26–29.

Johnstone, E.C., Crow, T.J., Frith, C.D., Husband, J., & Kreel, L. (1976). Cerebral ventricle size and cognitive impairment in chronic schizophrenia. *Lancet, ii,* 924–926.

Johnstone, E.C., Crow, T.J., Frith, C.D. Stevens, M., Kreel, L., & Husband, J. (1978a). The dementia of dementia praecox. *Acta Psychiatrica Scandinavica, 57,* 305–324.

Johnstone, E.C., Crow, T.J., Frith, C.D., Carney, M.W.P., & Price, J.S. (1978b). Mechanism of the antipsychotic effects in the treatment of acute schizophrenia. *Lancet, i,* 848–851.

Johnstone, E.C., Owens, D.G.C., Frith, C.D., & Calvert, L.M. (1985). Institutionalisation and the outcome of functional psychoses. *British Journal of Psychiatry, 146,* 36–44.

Johnstone, E.C., Crow, T.J., Frith, C.D., & Owens, D.G.C., (1988). The Northwick Park 'functional' psychosis study: Diagnosis and treatment response. *Lancet, ii,* 119–125.

Johnstone, E.C., Cooling, N.C., Frith, C.D., Crow, T.J., & Owens, D.G.C. (1988). Phenomenology of organic and functional psychoses and the overlap between them. *British Journal of Psychiatry, 153,* 770–776.

Jones-Gotman, M., & Milner, B. (1977). Design fluency: the invention of nonsense drawings after focal cortical lesions. *Neuropsychologia, 15,* 653–674.

Joseph, A.B. (1986). Focal central nervous system abnormalities in patients with misidentification syndromes. *Bibliotheca Psychiatrica, 164,* 68–79.

Jürgens, U. (1986). The squirrel monkey as an experimental model in the study of cerebral organisation of emotional vocal utterances. *European Archives of Psychiatry and Neurological Sciences, 236,* 4043.

Kaczmarek, B.L.J. (1987). Regulatory function of the frontal lobes: a neurolinguistic perspective. In E. Perecman (Ed.), *The frontal lobes revisited* (pp. 225–240) New York: IRBN Press.

Kandinskii, V. Kh. (1890). *O Pseudogallucinaciyach,* St. Petersburg.

Kapur, N., Turner, A., & King, C. (1988). Reduplicative paramnesia: Possible anatomical and neuropsychological mechanisms. *Journal of Neurology, Neurosurgery and Psychiatry, 51,* 579–581.

Kasinin, J., Knight, E., & Sage, P. (1934). The parent-child relationship in schizophrenia. *Journal of Nervous and Mental Diseases, 79,* 249–263.

Kertesz, A., & Shephard, A. (1981). The epidemiology of aphasic and cognitive impairments in stroke. *Brain, 104,* 117–128.

Kerwin, R. (Ed.) (1992). *Neurobiology and psychiatry (Vol.1).* Cambridge: Cambridge University Press.

Kirkpatrick, B., & Buchanan, R.W. (1990). The neural basis of the deficit syndrome in schizophrenia. *Journal of Nervous and Mental Disease, 178,* 545–555.

Kolb, B., & Wishaw, I.Q. (1983). Performance of schizophrenic patients on tests sensitive to left or right frontal, temporal or parietal function in neurological patients. *Journal of Nervous and Mental Disease, 171,* 435–443.

Kolb, B., & Wishaw, I.Q. (1985). *Fundamentals of human neuropsychology.* New York: W.H. Freeman.

Kraepelin, E. (1896). Dementia praecox. In J. Cutting & M. Shepherd (Eds. and Trans.), *The clinical routes of the schizophrenia concept.* Cambridge: Cambridge University Press.

Krawiecka, M., Goldberg, D., & Vaughan, M. (1977). A standardised psychiatric assessment for rating chronic psychotic patients. *Acta Psychiatrica Scandinavica, 55,* 299–308.

L'Abate, L., Boelling, G.M., Hutton, R.D., & Mather, D.L. (1962). The diagnostic usefulness of four potential tests of brain damage. *Journal of Consulting Psychology, 26,* 479.

Laborit, H., Huguenard, P., & Alluaume, R. (1952). Un nouveau stabilisateur vegetatif (le 4560.R.P). *Presse Medicine, 60,* 206–208.

Lancet editorial (1978). The biochemistry of depression. *Lancet, i,* 422–423.

Leach, J., & Wing, J.K. (1980). *Helping destitute men.* Tavistock: London.

Leff, J., & Abberton, E. (1981). Voice pitch measurements in schizophrenia and depression. *Psychological Medicine, 11,* 849–852.

Leslie, A.M. (1987). Pretence and representation: The origins of 'theory of mind'. *Psychological Review, 94,* 412-426.

Leudar, I., Thomas, P., & Johnstone, M. (submitted) Self-repair in dialogues of schizophrenics: effects of hallucinations and negative symptoms.

LeVine, W.R., & Conrad, R.L. (1979). The classification of schizophrenic neologisms. *Psychiatry, 42,* 177–181.

Lewine, R.R.J. (1985). Negative symptoms in schizophrenia: Editor's introduction. *Schizophrenia Bulletin, 11,* 361–363

Lhermitte, F. (1983). 'Utilisation behaviour' and its relation to lesions of the frontal lobes. *Brain, 106,* 237–255.

Liddle, P.F. (1987a). The symptoms of chronic schizophrenia: a reexamination of the positive-negative dichotomy. *British Journal of Psychiatry, 151,* 145–151.

Liddle, P.F. (1987b). Schizophrenic syndromes, cognitive performance and neurological dysfunction. *Psychological Medicine, 17,* 49–57.

Liddle, P.F., & Morris, D.L. (1991). Schizophrenic syndromes and frontal lobe performance. *British Journal of Psychiatry, 158,* 340–345.

Lishman, A.W. (1987). *Organic psychiatry.* Oxford: Blackwell.

Luria, A.R. (1973). *The working brain.* New York: Basic Books.

Lyon, M., & Robbins, T.W. (1975). The action of central nervous system stimulant drugs: a general theory concerning amphetamine effects. In W.B. Essman & L. Valzelli (Eds.), *Current developments in psychopharmacology* (vol. 2) (pp. 80–163) New York: Spectrum Publications.

Lyon, N., & Gerlach, J. (1988). Perseverative structuring of responses by schizophrenic patients and affective disorder patients. *Journal of Psychiatric Research, 20,* 137-150.

Lyon, N., Mejsholm, B., & Lyon, M. (1986). stereotyped responding by schizophrenic outpatients: cross-cultural confirmation of perseverative switching on a two-choice guessing task. *Journal of Psychiatric Research, 20,* 137–150.

Mackay, A.V.P., Iversen, L.L., Rossor, M., Spokes, E., Arregui, A., Creese, I., & Snyder, S.H. (1982). Increased brain dopamine and dopamine receptors in schizophrenia. *Archives of General Psychiatry, 39,* 992–997.

Macmillan, J.F. (1984). *The first schizophrenic illness: Presentation and short term outcome, incorporating a trial of prophylactic neuroleptic maintenance therapy versus placebo.* MD thesis, University of Edinburgh.

Maher, B. (1974). Delusional thinking and perceptual disorder. *Journal of Individual Psychology, 30,* 98–113.

Malenka, R.C., Angel, R.W., Hamptom, B., & Berger, P.A. (1982). Impaired central error correcting behaviour in schizophrenia. *Archives of General Psychiatry, 39,* 101–107.

Manschreck, T.C., Maher, B.A., Rucklos, M.E., & White, M.T. (1979). The predictabilityof thought disordered speech in schizophrenic patients. *British Journal of Psychiatry, 134,* 595–601.

Manschreck, T.C., Maher, B., Hoover, T.M., & Ames, D. (1984). The type-token ration in schizophrenic disorders:clinical and research value. *Psychological Medicine, 14,* 151–157.

Margo, A., Hemsley, D.R., & Slade, P.D. (1981). The effects of varying auditory input on schizophrenic hallucinations. *British Journal of Psychiatry, 139,* 122–127.

Marks, R.C., & Luchins, D.J. (1990). Relationship between brain imaging findings in schizophrenia and psychopathology: a review of the literature relating to positive and negative symptoms. In N. C. Andreasen (Ed.), *Modern problems of pharmacopsychiatry: Positive and negative symptoms and syndromes* (vol. 24). (pp. 89–123) Basel, Switzerland: S. Karger, A.G.

Marr, D. (1982). *Vision.* San Francisco: W.H. Freeman.

Marsden, C.D., Tarsy, D., & Baldessarini, R.J. (1975). Spontaneous and drug induced movement disorders in psychiatric patients. In D.F. Benson & D. Blumer (Eds.), *Psychiatric aspects of neurological disease* (pp. 219–266) New York: Grune & Stratton.

Marsden, C.D., Parkes, J.D., & Quinn, N. (1982). Fluctuations of disability in Parkinson's disease: Clinical aspects. In C.D. Marsden & S. Fahn (Eds.), *Movement disorders* (pp. 96–122) London: Butterworth.

Mazzoni, M., Pardossi, L., Cantini, R., Giorgetti, V., & Arena, R. (1990). Gerstmann syndrome: a case report. *Cortex, 26,* 459–467.

McCarthy, R.A., & Warrington, E.K. (1990). *Cognitive Neuropsychology.* London: Academic Press.

McGhie, A., & Chapman, J. (1961). Disorders of attention and perception in early schizophrenia. *British Journal of Psychiatry, 34,* 103–116.

McGrath, J. (1991). Ordering thoughts on thought disorder. *British Journal of Psychiatry, 158,* 307–316.

McGuigan, F.J. (1966). Covert oral behaviour and auditory hallucinations. *Psychophysiology, 3,* 73–80.

McKenna, P.J., Tamlyn, D., Lund, C.E., Mortimer, A.M., Hammond, S., & Baddeley, A.D. (1990). Amnesic syndrome in schizophrenia. *Psychological Medicine, 20,* 967–972.

McPherson, F.M., Barden, V., Hay, A.J., Johnstone, D.W., & Kushner, A.W. (1970). Flattening of affect and personal constructs. *British Journal of Psychiatry, 116,* 39–43.

Megaw, E.D. (1972). Directional errors and their correction in a discrete tracking task. *Ergonomics, 15,* 633–643.

Mesulam, M-M. (1990). Large-scale neurocognitive networks and distributed processing for attention, language, and memory. *Annals of Neurology, 28,* 597–613.

Miller, E. (1984). Verbal fluency as a function of a measure of verbal intelligence and in relation to different types of cerebral pathology. *British Journal of Clinical Psychology, 23,* 53–57.

Miller, J.G. (1960). Information input overload and psychopathology. *American Journal of Psychiatry, 116,* 695–704.

Milner, A.D., Perrett, D.I., Johnstone, R.S., Benson, P.J., Jordan, T.R., Heeley, D.W., Bettucci, D., Mortana, F., Mutani, R., Terazzi, E., & Davidson, D.L.W. (1991). Perception and Action in 'visual form agnosia'. *Brain, 114,* 405–428.

Montague, R.L., Tantam, D., Newby, D., Thomas, P., & Ring, N. (1989). The incidence of negative symptoms in early schizophrenia, mania and other psychoses. *Acta Psychiatrica Scandanavica, 79,* 613–618.

Morice, R. (1986). The structure, organisation, and use of language in schizophrenia. In Burrows, O., Norman, P., & Rubenstein, T. (Eds.), *Handbook of studies on schizophrenia. Part I.* Amsterdam: Elsevier.

Morice, R. (1990). Cognitive inflexibility and pre-frontal dysfunction in schizophrenia and mania. *British Journal of Psychiatry, 157,* 50–54.

Morice, R.D., & Ingram, J.C.L. (1982). Language analysis in schizophrenia: Diagnostic implications. *Australian and New Zealand Journal of Psychiatry, 16,* 11–21.

Mortimer, A.M., Lund, C.E., & McKenna, P.J. (1990). The positive: negative dichotomy in schizophrenia. *British Journal of Psychiatry, 157,* 41–49.

Morton, J. (1984). Brain-based and non-brain based models of language. In D. Caplan, A.R. Lecours, & A. Smith (Eds.), *Biological perspectives in language.* Cambridge, Mass.: MIT Press.

Müller-Preuss, P., & Jürgens, U. (1976). Projections from the 'cingular' vocalisation area in the squirrel monkey. *Brain Research, 103,* 29–43.

Müller-Preuss, P. (1978). Single unit responses of the auditory cortex in the squirrel monkey to self-produced and loudspeaker transmitted vocalisations. *Neuroscience Letters, Supplement 1*, S. 7.

Müller-Preuss, P., Newman, J.D., & Jürgens, U. (1980). Evidence for an anatomic and physiological relationship between the 'cingular' vocalisation area and the auditory cortex in the squirrel monkey. *Brain Research, 202*, 307-315.

Murphy, D., & Cutting, J. (1990). Prosodic comprehension and expression in schizophrenia. *Journal of Neurology, Neurosurgery and Psychiatry, 53*, 727-730.

Murray, R.M., & Lewis, S.W. (1987). Is schizophrenia a developmental disorder? *British Medical Journal, 295*, 681-682.

Nasrallah, H.A. (1991). Magnetic resonance imaging of the brain: Clinical and research application in schizophrenia. In H. Hafner & W.F. Gattaz (Eds.), *Search for the causes of schizophrenia (vol II)*. Berlin: Springer.

O'Callaghan, E., Larkin, C., Redmond, O., Stack, J., Ennis, J.T., & Waddington, J. (1988). 'Early onset schizophrenia' after teenage head injury. *British Journal of Psychiatry, 153*, 394-396.

Owen, F., Cross, A.J., Crow, T.J., Longden, A., Poulter, M., & Riley, G.J. (1978). Increased dopamine-receptor sensitivity in schizophrenia. *Lancet, ii*, 223-226.

Owens, D.G.C., & Johnstone, E.C. (1980). The disabilities of chronic schizophrenia"their nature and the factors contributing to their development. *British Journal of Psychiatry, 136*, 384-395.

Owens, D.G.C., Johnstone, E.C., & Frith, C.D. (1982). Spontaneous involuntary disorders of movement. *Archives of General Psychiatry, 39*, 452-461.

Owens, D.G.C., Johnstone, E.C., Crow, T.J., Frith, C.D., Jagoe, J.R., & Kreel, L. (1985). Lateral ventricle size in schizophrenia: relation to the disease process and its clinical manifestations. *Psychological Medicine, 15*, 27-41.

Pakkenberg, B. (1987). Post mortem study of chronic schizophrenic brains. *British Journal of Psychiatry, 151*, 744-752.

Passingham, R.E. (1987). Two cortical systems for directing movement. In *Motor areas of the cerebral cortex* Ciba Foundation Symposium 132 (pp. 151-161) Chichester: Wiley.

Passingham, R.E., Chen, Y.C., & Thaler, D. (1989). Supplementary motor cortex and self-initiated movement. In M. Ito (Ed.), *Neural programming*. Basel: Karger.

Perner, J. (1991). *Understanding the representational mind*. Cambridge, Mass: MIT Press.

Perner, J., Frith, U., Leslie, A.M., & Leekham, S.R. (1989). Exploration of the autistic child's theory of mind: Knowledge, belief and communication. *Child Development, 60*, 689-700.

Perret, E. (1974). The left frontal lobe of man and the suppression of habitual responses in verbal categorical behaviour. *Neuropsychologia, 12*, 323-330.

Perret, D.I., Mistlin, A.J., Potter, D.D., Smith, P.A.J., Head, A.S., Chitty, A.J., Broenimann, R., Milner, A.D., & Jeeves, M.A. (1986). Functional organisation of visual neurones processing face identity. In H. Ellis, M.A. Jeeves, F. Newcombe, & A.W. Young (Eds.). *Aspects of face processing*. (pp. 187-198). Dordrecht: Martinus Nijhoff.

Petersen, S.E., Fox, P.T., Posner, M.I., Mintun, M & Raichle, M.E. (1989). Positron emission tomographic studies of the processing of single words. *Journal of Cognitive Neuroscience, 1*, 153-170.

Petty, L.K., Ornitz, E.M., Michelman, J.D., & Zimmerman, E.G. (1984). Autistic children who become schizophrenic. *Archives of General Psychiatry, 41,* 129-135.

Piaget, J. (1936/1953). *The origin of intelligence in the child.* London: Routledge & Kegan Paul.

Pilowsky, I., & Bassett, D. (1980). Schizophrenia and the response to facial emotions. *Comprehensive Psychiatry, 21,* 236-244.

Ploog, D. (1979). Phonation, emotion, cognition: with reference to the brain mechanisms involved. In *Brain and mind* CIBA Foundation Symposium 69 (pp. 79-98). Amsterdam: Elsevier/North-Holland.

Plum, F. (1972). Prospects for research on schizophrenia. 3. Neurophysiology. Neuropathological findings. *Neurosciences Research Program, Bulletin 10,* 384-388.

Popper, K.R., & Eccles, J.C. (1977). *The self and its brain* (2nd ed.). London: Routledge & Kegan Paul.

Premack, D., & Woodruff, G. (1978). Does the chimpanzee have a theory of mind? *Behavioural and Brain Sciences, 4,* 515-526.

Rabbitt, P.M.A. (1966). Error-correction time without external signals. *Nature, 212,* 438.

Raleigh, M.J., & Stelkis, H.D. (1981). Effects of orbitofrontal and temporal neocortical lesions on the affiliative behaviour of vervet monkeys. *Experimental Neurology, 73,* 378-389.

Randrup, A., & Munkvad, I. (1972). Evidence indicating an association between schizophrenia and dopaminergic hyperactivity in the brain. *Orthomolecular Psychiatry, 1,* 2-7.

Ridley, R.M., & Baker, H.F. (1983). Is there a relationship between social isolation, cognitive inflexibility, and behavioural stereotypy? An analysis of the effects of amphetamine in the marmoset. In *Ethopharmacology: Primate models of neuropsychiatric disorders.* New York: Alan Liss.

Ridley, R.M., Baker, H.F., Frith, C.D., Dowdy, J., & Crow, T.J. (1988). Stereotyped responding on a two-choice guessing task by marmosets and humans treated with amphetamine. *Psychopharmacology, 95,* 560-564.

Ridley, R.M., & Baker, H.F. (1991). A critical evaluation of monkey models of amnesia and dementia. *Brain Research Reviews, 16,* 15-37.

Robbins, T.W. (1982). Stereotypies: Addictions or fragmented actions? *Bulletin of the British Psychological Society, 35,* 297-300.

Robbins, T.W. (1990). The case for a frontostriatal dysfunction in schizophrenia. *Schizophrenia Bulletin, 16,* 391-402.

Roberts, G.W., & Bruton, C.J. (1990).Notes from the graveyard: Schizophrenia and neuropathology. *Neuropathology and Applied Neurobiology, 16,* 3-16.

Robinson, D.L., & Wurtz, R.H. (1976). Use of an extraretinal signal by monkey superior colliculus neurons to distinguish real from self-induced movement. *Journal of Neurophysiology, 39,* 852-870.

Rochester, S., & Martin, J.R. (1979). *Crazy talk: A study of the discourse of schizophrenic speakers.* New York: Plenum Press.

Rosenberg, S., & Cohen, B. (1966). Referential processes of speakers and listeners. *Psychological Review, 73,* 208-231.

Ruocchio, P.J. (1991). First person account: The schizophrenic inside. *Schizophrenia Bulletin, 17,* 357-359.

Rutter, D.R. (1985). Language in schizophrenia: the structure of monologues and conversations. *British Journal of Psychiatry, 146,* 399–404.

Salzinger, K. Portnoy, S., & Feldman, R.S. (1978). Communicability deficit in schizophrenics resulting from a more general deficit. In S. Schwartz (Ed.), *Language and cognition in schizophrenia* (pp. 35–53) Hillsdale, N.J.: Lawrence Erlbaum Associates Inc.

Saravay, S.M., & Pardes, H. (1967). Auditory elementary hallucinations in alcohol withdrawal psychoses. *Archives of General Psychiatry, 16,* 652–658.

Schneider, K. (1959). *Clinical Psychopathology.* New York: Grune & Stratton.

Schopler, E., & Mesibov, G.E. (Eds.) (1988). *Diagnosis and Assessment in Autism.* New York: Plenum Press.

Schröder, P. (1926). Das Halluzinieren. *Zeitschrift für die gesamte Neurologie und Psychiatrie, Berlin, 101,* 599–614.

Seeman, P., Lee, T., Chau-Wong, M., & Wong, K. (1976). Antipsychotic drug doses and neuroleptic/dopamine receptors. *Nature (London), 261,* 717–719.

Shakow, D. (1950). Some psychological features of schizophrenia. In M.L. Reymert (Ed.), *Feelings and emotions* (pp. 383–390) New York: McGraw Hill.

Shallice, T. (1988). *From neuropsychology to mental structure.* Cambridge: Cambridge University Press.

Shallice, T., & Jackson, M. (1988). Lissauer on agnosia. *Cognitive Neuropsychology, 5,* 153–192.

Shallice, T., Burgess, P., & Frith, C.D. (1991). Can the neuropsychological case-study approach be applied to schizophrenia? *Psychological Medicine, 21,* 661–673.

Shultz, T.R., Wells, D., & Sarda, M. (1980). The development of the ability to distinguish intended actions from mistakes, reflexes and passive movements. *The British Journal of Social and Clinical Psychology, 19,* 301–310.

Slade, P.D., & Bentall, R.P. (1988). *Sensory deception: A scientific analysis of hallucination.* London: Croom Helm.

Sperber, D., & Wilson, D. (1986). *Relevance: communication and cognition.* Oxford: Blackwell.

Sperry, R.W. (1950). Neural basis of the spontaneous optokinetic response produced by visual inversion. *Journal of Comparative and Physiological Psychology, 43,* 482–489.

Spohn, H.E., & Strauss, M.E. (1989). Relation of neuroleptic and anticholinergic medication to cognitive function in schizophrenia. *Journal of Abnormal Psychology, 98,* 367–380.

Sterne, L. (1760). *The life and opinions of Tristram Shandy.* London: Dodsley.

Stevens, M., Crow, T.J., Bowman, M.J., & Coles, E.C. (1978). Age disorientation in schizophrenia: a constant prevalence of about 25% in a chronic mental hospital population? *British Journal of Psychiatry, 133,* 130–136.

Thomas, P., King, K., Fraser, W., & Kendell, R.E. (1987). Linguistic performance in schizophrenia: a comparison of patients with positive and negative symptoms. *Acta Psychiatrica Scandinavica, 76,* 144–151.

Trimble, M.R. (1990). First-rank symptoms of Schneider. A new perspective? *British Journal of Psychiatry, 156,* 195–200.

Volkmar, F., Cohen, D., & Paul, R. (1986). An evaluation of DSM-III criteria for infantile autism. *Journal of the American Academy of Child Psychiatry, 25,* 190–197.

Warren, R.M. (1970). Perceptual restoration of missing speech sounds. *Science, 167*, 392–393.

Watkins, J.M., Asarnow, R.F., & Tanguay, P.E. (1988). Symptom development in childhood onset schizophrenia. *Journal of Child Psychology & Psychiatry, 29*, 865–878.

Waugh, E. (1957). *The ordeal of Gilbert Pinfold*. London: Chapman and Hall.

Weinberger, D.R. (1984). Computed tomography (CT) findings in schizophrenia: speculation on the meaning of it all. *Journal of Psychiatric Research, 18*, 477–490.

Weinberger, D.R. (1988). Premorbid neuropathology in schizophrenia. *Lancet, ii*, 959–960.

Weinberger, D.R., Bigelow, L.L.B., Kleinman, J.E., Klein, S.T., Rosenblatt, J.E., & Wyatt, R.J. (1980). Cerebral ventricular enlargement in chronic schizophrenia: an association with poor response to treatment. *Archives of General Psychiatry, 37*, 11–13.

Weiner, I., Lubow, R., & Feldon, J. (1981). Chronic amphetamine and latent inhibition. *Behavioural and Brain Science, 2*, 285–286.

Weiskrantz, L. (1980). Varieties of residual experience. *Quarterly Journal of Experimental Psychology, 32*, 365–386.

Weiskrantz, L. (1987). Neuropsychology and the nature of consciousness. In C. Blakemore & S. Greenfield (Eds.), *Mindwaves* (pp. 307–320). Oxford: Blackwell.

Wing, J.K. (1976). Impairments in schizophrenia: A rational basis for treatment. In R.D. Wirt, G. Winokur & M. Roff, (Eds.), *Life history research in psychopathology* (vol. 4). (pp. 238–268) Minneapolis: University of Minnesota Press.

Wing, J.K., & Brown, G.W. (1970). *Institutionalism and schizophrenia*. London: Cambridge University Press.

Wing, L., & Gould, J. (1979). Severe impairments of social interaction and associated abnormalities in children: Epidemiology and classification. *Journal of Autism and Developmental Disorders, 9*, 11–30.

Wing, J.K., & Wing, L. (1982). *Handbook of Psychiatry, (vol. 3). Psychoses of uncertain aetiology*. Cambridge: Cambridge University Press.

Wing, J.K., Birley, J.L.T., Cooper, J.D., Graham, P., & Isaacs, A.D. (1967). Reliability of a procedure for measuring and classifying present psychiatric state. *British Journal of Psychiatry, 113*, 499–515.

Wing, J.K., Cooper, J.E., & Sartorius, N. (1974). *Description and classification of psychiatric symptoms*. London: Cambridge University Press.

Wise, R., Chouet, F., Hadar, U., Friston, K., Hoffner, E., Frackowiak, R.S.J. (1991). Distribution of cortical neuronal networks involved in word comprehension and word retrieval. *Brain, 114*, 1803-1817.

Wolfe, N., Katz, D.I., Albert, M.L. et al., (1990). Neuropsychological profile linked to low dopamine: in Alzheimer's disease, major depression and Parkinson's disease. *Journal of Neurology, Neurosurgery and Psychiatry, 53*, 915–917.

Wong, D.F., Wagner, H.N., Tune, L.E., Dannals, R.F., Pearlsson, G.D., Links, J.M., Tamminga, C.A., Broussole, E.P., Ravert, H.T., Wilson, A.A., Toung, J.K., Malat, J., Williams, F.A., O'Touma, L.A., Snyder, S.H., Kuhar, M.J., & Gjedde, A. (1986). Positron emission tomography reveals elevated D2 dopamine receptors in drug-naive schizophrenic patients. *Science, 234*, 1558–1563.

World Health Organization (1975). *Schizophrenia: A multinational study.* Geneva: WHO.

Wykes, T., & Leff, J. (1982). Disordered speech: Differences between manics and schizophrenics. *Brain and Language, 15,* 117–124.

Zeki, S. (1978). Functional specialisation in the visual cortex of the rhesus monkey. *Nature, 274,* 423–428.

Zuckerman, M. (1969) Variables affecting deprivation results. In J.P. Zubeck (Ed.), *Sensory deprivation.* New York: Appleton-Century-Crofts.

Author Index

Subject Index

Also of interest.....

THE NEUROPSYCHOLOGY OF SCHIZOPHRENIA

ANTHONY DAVID (King's College Hospital), JOHN CUTTING (Bethlem Royal Hospital) Eds.

Schizophrenia is being increasingly viewed as a neurological disorder. The Neuropsychology of Schizophrenia addresses the key questions in modern schizophrenia research. How do abnormalities of the brain produce the characteristic signs and symptoms of this most severe and mysterious mental malady? Where are these abnormalities? How do they develop? How can we detect them? What clinical and cognitive effects do they have?

This new book is the first of its kind to tackle these questions in a systematic way from a number of allied perspectives: from phenomenology to physiology, animal behaviour to metacognition and from PET scans to paper and pencil tests.

Contents: A.S. David, J. Cutting, The Neuropsychology of Schizophrenia: Introduction and Overview. Part I: *Neuroimaging and Neuropsychology.* T. Early, J.W. Haller, M.I. Posner, M. Raichle, The Left Striato-Pallidal Hyperactivity Model of Schizophrenia. P. Liddle, Volition and Schizophrenia. Part II: *Information Processing.* K.H. Nuechterlein, M.S. Buchsbaum, M.E. Dawson, Neuropsychological Vulnerability to Schizophrenia. M.F. Green, K.H. Nuechterlein, Mechanisms of Backward Masking in Schizophrenia. D. Hemsley, Perceptual and Cognitive Abnormalities as the Bases for Schizophrenic Symptoms. Part III: *Neuropsychology and Neurodevelopment.* E. Walker, Neuro-developmental Precursors of Schizophrenia. P. Jones, C. Guth, S. Lewis, R. Murray, Low Intelligence and Poor Education Achievement Precede early Onset Schizophrenic Psychosis. Part IV: *Cognition and Metacognition.* C. Frith, Theory of Mind in Schizophrenia. P.J. McKenna, A.M. Mortimer, J.R. Hodges, Semantic Memory in Schizophrenia. Part V: *Clinical Neuropsychology.* G. Dunkley, D. Rogers, The Cognitive Impairment of Severe Psychiatric Illness. K. Fleming, T.E. Goldberg, J.M. Gold, Applying Working Memory Constructs to Schizophrenic Cognitive Impairment. C. Panelis, H. Nelson, Cognitive Functioning and Symptomatology in Schizophrenia: The Role of Fronto-Subcortical Involvement. J. Cutting, Evidence for Right Hemisphere Dysfunction in Schizophrenia. Part VI: *Auditory Hallucinations.* P. Slade, Models of Hallucination: From Theory to Practice. R. Hoffman, J. Rapaport, A Psycholinguistic Study of Auditory/Verbal Hallucinations: Preliminary Findings. Part VII: *Delusions and Delusional Misidentification.* A.S. David, The Neuropsychological Origin of Auditory Hallucinations. H.D. Ellis, K.W. de Pauw, The Cognitive Neuropsychiatric Origins of the Capgras Delusion. R.B. Bentall, Biases and Abnormal Beliefs: Towards a Model of Persecutory Delusions. S. Fleminger, Top-Down Preconscious Perceptual Processing and Delusional Misidentification in Neuropsychiatric Disorder.

ISBN 0-86377-303-6 1994 400pp. $65.95 £35.00 hbk
Brain Damage, Behaviour, and Cognition Series.

LAWRENCE ERLBAUM ASSOCIATES